# IDIOM DRILLS

D0062175

# IDIOM DRILLS

## FOR STUDENTS OF ENGLISH AS A SECOND LANGUAGE

### GEORGE P. McCALLUM

*English Department*
International Institute in Spain

THOMAS Y. CROWELL COMPANY
New York   Established 1834

THOMAS Y. CROWELL COMPANY
666 FIFTH AVENUE
NEW YORK, N.Y. 10019

# PREFACE

This series of idiom exercises is designed to help foreign students of English master 180 useful everyday idioms. It is divided into six units, with five individual lessons in each unit. At the end of each unit is a short reading, which incorporates all thirty of the idioms studied in that unit.

The idioms included in this collection were selected on the basis of frequency of usage, although this by no means indicates that these are the 180 most-used idioms in American English. A conscious effort was made, however, to employ only those expressions currently used generally throughout the United States and to exclude regional expressions and slang.

Each lesson contains six new idioms, with brief definitions and illustrations. These idioms are drilled by means of a short dialogue, substitution drills, and simple homework exercises. Most of the dialogues are written so that male and female students may take either role.

These are purposely short lessons; they are meant to be supplements, a brief rest from the regular lessons. Approximately fifteen minutes of classroom time each day should be spent in going over a new lesson. The following day, before taking up the next lesson, the instructor might spend a few minutes reviewing the previous day's homework. They are primarily oral exercises.

The lessons are not aimed at any particular level, although it is believed they will be especially useful to students at the intermediate and advanced levels.

Taking twenty minutes a day, a class should be able to complete this series of drills in a six-week intensive course. A teacher may find that with certain classes it is advisable to use these drills less frequently; the time involved with other basic materials should dictate this.

The reading at the end of each unit is designed as a homework assignment, being a review of the idioms studied in that unit. The questions at the end of each reading may be answered as written homework or can be the basis of a class discussion on the reading.

Special thanks for their helpful suggestions are due John A. Floyd, Director of the ELS Language Center, Washington, D.C., where these drills were tested over a year's time, and the following instructors: Jeanne Birnbaum, Irene Dutra, Dorothea Erenreich, William Goble, Richard Sackett, Anabelle Scoon, Ray Valdivia, John Washburn and Leonard Weiss.

G. P. M.

# CONTENTS

# UNIT II

viii

# UNIT III

# UNIT IV

on hand | little does one think | keep one's fingers crossed

# UNIT V

# UNIT VI

# UNIT I

## DRILL 1

### DIALOGUE

A: Let's go to the movies. There's a good picture at the Roxy.

B: I'd like to, but I can't. I have to study. I wasted the whole afternoon. I forgot I had to **brush up on** my French. Then, **all of a sudden,** I remembered.

A: Oh, come on! We'll be home early.

B: No, **I'd better** not. I have an exam tomorrow. I was **about to** study when you came in. You know how it is. If you don't study, you don't pass. That **goes without saying.**

A: Exam? Tomorrow? Oh-oh!

B: **What's the matter?**

A: I just remembered. I have an exam, too!

B: We can go to the movies on Saturday.

### DEFINITIONS

**brush up on something**   review something to make it fresh again in one's mind

1

*I'm going to give a speech tomorrow, so I have to brush up on my notes.*

**all of a sudden**  something happening quickly; without advance warning
*It started out to be a beautiful day. Then, all of a sudden, it became cloudy and began to rain.*

**had better ('d better)**  should do something; ought to do something
*I'd better go now or I'll be late for class.*

**about to**  on the point of doing something
*Tom was about to leave when the telephone rang.*

**goes without saying**  something is so obvious that it doesn't have to be mentioned
*Mary's an excellent student. It goes without saying that her parents are very proud of her.*

**What's the matter?**  What is wrong?
*What's the matter with Alice? She looks angry.*


## SUBSTITUTION DRILL

*Repeat the following sentences, using the substitutions listed.*

1.  I have to brush up on my French.
    > my English.
    > mathematics.
    > history.
    > grammar rules.
    > chemistry.
    > botany.

2.  All of a sudden I remembered.
    > she left the room.
    > it began to rain.

2

Eva started to cry.
Frank became angry.
Harry began to laugh.
Jean wanted to leave.

3. I'd better not go to the movies tonight.
   tell Jane what happened.
   eat supper now.
   lose those papers.
   fail the examination.
   forget to buy stamps.
   sell my car.

4. I was about to study when you came in.
   go when the phone rang.
   write her a letter when she arrived.
   tell them a story when they walked away.
   eat supper when John called me.
   play the piano when the doorbell rang.
   call my dog when he ran into the house.

5. It goes without saying that we must study hard.
   haste makes waste.
   a penny saved is a penny
     earned.
   many hands make light work.
   you're as old as you feel.
   education is important.
   good health is essential.

6. What's the matter? You look angry.
   John looks tired.
   Your arm is bleeding.
   Mary's shouting.
   The baby is crying.
   George is running.
   You're trembling.

## HOMEWORK EXERCISE

*Rewrite the following sentences, substituting an idiom for the italicized section of the sentence.*

1. Bill looked very sad, but then, *without advance warning,* he began to sing.
2. Mary was *on the point of leaving* when Mrs. Allen invited her to stay for lunch.
3. Professor Smith had not given a talk on Shakespeare for a long time, so he had to *review* some of the plays.
4. *"What's wrong,* Fred?" asked Jean. "You look like you don't feel well."
5. Anne just told me she can't go with us. *Obviously* we're disappointed.
6. You *should* take your raincoat, because it's supposed to rain today.

# DRILL 2

## DIALOGUE

A: **Every now and then** I get hungry for French food.

B: There's a good French restaurant near here. Let's go sometime.

A: Why not tonight?

B: No, not tonight. You have to make reservations **in advance.** It's a very popular place. Besides, it's expensive. And I don't have any money.

A: **I'm broke,** too. Let's save our money and go next week.

B: Okay. But how?

A: We could **do without** lunch this week.

B: Do you mean every day? I don't **feel up to** that.

A: Well, then **every other** day.

## DEFINITIONS

**every now and then**   occasionally
> *Every now and then I like to take a walk in the country.*

**in advance**   before; ahead of time
> *If you want to see that play, you should buy your tickets in advance.*

**be broke**   be without money
> *I'd like to go to the concert with you, but I'm broke.*

**do without**   live without something
> *If there's no butter for our bread, we'll do without.*

**feel up to**   feel able (health or ability) to do something
> *I ought to go to Jane's party, but I just don't feel up to it now.*

**every other**   alternate
> *This class meets every other day, not every day.*


## SUBSTITUTION DRILL

*Repeat the following sentences, using the substitutions listed.*

1.   Every now and then I get hungry for French food.
> John goes to New York.
> Mary gives a party.
> Henry likes to play cards.
> we speak Chinese to each other.
> the weather gets quite cold.
> the Smiths give a big dinner.

2.   You can make reservations in advance.
> We bought our tickets
> They gave us the information
> The teacher told us our grades

Jim gave Anne her birthday gift
I ought to send a telegram
She's going to phone us

3. I'm broke this week.
John's
We're
He's
Ellen's
They're
Tom's

4. We could do without lunch this week.
breakfast today.
supper tonight.
cream in our coffee.
butter on the bread.
dessert every day.
jelly on our toast.

5. I don't feel up to eating any dessert.
going to the concert.
participating in the play.
giving a speech today.
driving to Chicago.
arguing with my wife.
playing bridge tonight.

6. Let's do without lunch every other day.
walk to work
go to the library
play golf
study together
practice French
go swimming

## HOMEWORK EXERCISE

*Write an original sentence with each of the following idioms:*

| | |
|---|---|
| be broke | do without |
| every other | every now and then |
| feel up to | in advance |

# DRILL 3

## DIALOGUE

A: Have you heard that Jane cancelled her party next Friday?

B: Yes, but I didn't hear why. What happened?

A: She's going to New York. She has to **see about something** for her boss.

B: Why did Jane plan the party? She knew **all along** about New York, didn't she?

A: Yes, but she really **isn't to blame.** She thought the trip would be next week. Yesterday she was told to go this week.

B: Too bad about the party, **to say the least.** The trip will **do Jane good,** though.

A: And she can have the party when she returns.

B: Frankly, I'm glad about the party. I'm **up to my ears** in work right now.

## DEFINITIONS

**see about**   take the responsibilty to do something; make arrangements for

*Let's have a picnic on Sunday. I'll **see about** the food.*

**all along**   all the time
> *I knew **all along** that Jack wasn't telling us the whole story.*

**be to blame**   be responsible for something bad or unfortunate
> *Don't punish Billy for breaking the window. He's not **to blame**.*

**to say the least**   to make the minimum comment about something or someone
> *It's a boring novel, **to say the least**.*

**do someone good**   be beneficial for someone
> *Go to the seashore for a few days; the fresh air will **do you good**.*

**be up to one's ears**   have too much to do
> *Helen would like to go with us but she can't. She's **up to her ears** in work.*


## SUBSTITUTION DRILL

*Repeat the following sentences, using the substitutions listed.*

1.   She has to see about something for her boss.
> some business in Chicago.
> that house on Elm Street.
> a gift for her mother.
> an appointment this afternoon.
> a ride downtown.
> a contract for her company.

2.   She knew all along about the trip to New York.
> our party.
> Jim's letter.
> the accident.

his plans.
her uncle.
your request.

3.    She really isn't to blame for the change.
                                 the error.
                                 our problem.
                                 the fire.
                                 what happened.
                                 being late.
                                 losing the tickets.

4.    The trip will do Jane good, though.
    The change
    The comedy
    Your visit
    That book
    My plan
    That course

5.    Too bad about the party, to say the least.
    I'm sorry you can't come,
    We're grateful that you told us,
    Jim regrets what he said,
    I appreciate knowing the facts,
    She's a fine wife and mother,
    He has a good picture of the case,

6.    I'm up to my ears in work right now.
    Jim's
    They're
    Joan's
    We're
    She's
    Bill's

## HOMEWORK EXERCISE

*Choose the correct idiom from the lesson to complete these sentences.*

1. I'm going to the kitchen. I have to _____ the coffee.
2. You shouldn't talk that way about Barbara. She _____ _____ for what happened last night.
3. Why don't you take a vacation? The rest will _____.
4. The Smiths are going to build a new house. Right now they're _____ in plans and blueprints.
5. I don't know why Henry didn't tell us before. He knew _____that Alice wouldn't be here tonight.
6. I'm sorry about what happened, Jack, _____. I know it wasn't your fault.

# DRILL 4

## DIALOGUE

A: Will you **keep an eye on** my books? I'll be back in five minutes.

B: Where are you going? **Are you up to something?** You look as though you are.

A: Not really. But here comes Dorothy. I'd **just as soon** she didn't see me.

B: Why not?

A: She **had her heart set on** seeing a movie. I promised to take her. Then I discovered I didn't have any money. I phoned her and said I was sick.

B: Relax. She's going out the other door. You're safe **for the time being.**

A: That was **a close call.**

# DEFINITIONS

**keep an eye on something, someone**   watch in the sense of take care of

> *Will you keep an eye on my baby while I go to the store?*

**be up to something**   doing something that one shouldn't do

> *Henry's been smiling to himself all morning. I think he's up to something, but I don't know what it is.*

**just as soon**   prefer that one thing be done rather than another

> *My wife wants to attend that lecture, but I'd just as soon stay home.*

**have one's heart set on something**   want something very much

> *I don't know what to do. My wife has her heart set on a new coat for her birthday, but I don't have enough money to buy it.*

**for the time being**   for the present time

> *I need a new car, but for the time being this one will have to do.*

**a close call**   a situation in which something bad almost happened

> *I had a close call! A big truck almost hit me!*


## SUBSTITUTION DRILL

*Repeat the following sentences, using the substitutions listed.*

1.   Will you keep an eye on my books?

> my children?
>
> the class?

the students?
our car?
my dog?
Jim's cat?

2.   Where are you going? Are you up to something?
     What are you doing?
     Who are you calling?
     Who are you writing to?
     Why are you laughing?
     Why are you smiling?
     What are you drawing?

3.   I'd just as soon she didn't see me.
                    they didn't find me.
                    Tom didn't telephone.
                    you didn't ask him.
                    he didn't invite us.
                    we didn't go tonight.
                    it didn't snow today.

4.   She had her heart set on seeing a movie.
                         going swimming.
                         buying a new hat.
                         attending the concert.
                         eating at that restaurant.
                         going with them.
                         playing golf today.

5.   You're safe for the time being.
          all right
          healthy
          rich
          accepted
          lucky
          eligible

6.    That was a close call I had.

> you
> Mary
> Bill
> we
> Alex
> Bob

## HOMEWORK EXERCISE

*Answer the following questions, using complete sentences.*

1. Have you had a close call recently?
2. Why is it necessary to keep an eye on little children?
3. If you saw a man climbing into your neighbor's window, would you think he was up to something?
4. If you were asked to choose, would you go to a symphony concert or would you just as soon go to a movie?
5. Have you ever had your heart set on something and then been disappointed?
6. Do you have enough money for the time being?

# DRILL 5

## DIALOGUE

A:    Come in, please. **Make yourself at home.**

B:    Thanks. You have a nice place here.

A:    I'm glad you like it. The furniture's in pretty bad condition, though. We should **get rid of it.**

B:    Don't do that. It's very comfortable. You have children, don't you?

A:   Yes, we do. Three boys and a girl. **Not to mention** two dogs. So we have to **make this furniture do. As long as** the children are small, anyway.

B:   I know what you mean. Our children are **hard on** furniture, too.


## DEFINITIONS

**make oneself at home**   be comfortable, as if in one's own home

> *When people come to our house, we like them **to make themselves at home**.*

**get rid of something**   destroy; throw away; sell

> *When Ella told Frank she didn't like his hat, he **got rid of it**.*

**not to mention**   omitting to say anything about something

> *I can't go to Steve's party. I've got to do my homework, prepare a speech for tomorrow, and study for an exam, **not to mention** take my little brother to the dentist.*

**make something do**   use what one has instead of getting something else that would be better

> *If there isn't cream for our coffee, **we'll have to make milk do**.*

**be hard on something**   treat roughly

> *My son **is hard on** shoes. Look at this pair. These were new a month ago.*

**as long as**   because something else is happening at the same time

> ***As long as** you're going to the drugstore anyway, buy me some aspirins.*

# SUBSTITUTION DRILL

*Repeat the following sentences, using the substitutions listed.*

1. Come in. Make yourself at home.
   Sit down.
   Take off your coat.
   Let me take your hat.
   Have a chair.
   Look around.
   Have a cigarette.

2. We should get rid of the furniture.
   those curtains.
   this sofa.
   these lamps.
   that table.
   this rug.
   those chairs.

3. We have three children, not to mention two dogs.
   four cats.
   ten goldfish.
   five grand-
   children.
   two horses.
   twenty canaries.
   six kittens.

4. We have to make this furniture do.
   this rug
   these chairs
   that sofa
   those lamps
   this car
   these pictures

5. As long as the children are small, we can't travel.

> we won't buy furniture.
> I won't work.
> I'll teach them at home.
> Mary stays home.
> we must take care of them.
> we have a lot to do.

6. Our children are hard on furniture.

> shoes.
> clothes.
> our nerves.
> each other.
> their toys.
> everything.

## HOMEWORK EXERCISE

*Rewrite these sentences, substituting an idiom where possible.*

1. While Bobby is in elementary school, we want to remain in this neighborhood.
2. I'm going to throw out these curtains. I don't like them any more.
3. Come in and sit down. Please be comfortable.
4. I don't like to give my nephew toys for Christmas. He doesn't take care of them.
5. Jim didn't want to go to the movies because he had to study, without talking about the fact that he doesn't have any money.
6. The Browns wanted a new sofa but decided to continue using the old one for another year.

# READING I

## THE ABSENTMINDED PROFESSOR

Every afternoon when Professor Herbert Allen walked home from the university, he was so occupied with the book in his hand that he never saw anything around him. When he reached home, his wife would say, "What happened today, Herbert?" and he would answer, "Nothing."

The truth was that if anything did happen, he didn't know it. He was much too busy **brushing up on** Voltaire, Hegel, or some other philosopher. Still, he gave his wife the same answer every day. She knew **in advance** that he would, but she asked anyway.

One day, however, Herbert had a different answer ready for his wife. It was all because of the weather. That afternoon the spring weather was so beautiful that he left the university earlier than usual and went to the park. Of course, he carried a philosophy book in his hand. **As long as** he had to read this book anyway, why not in the park? He sat down on a bench under a tree, **made himself at home** there, and started to read. Around him were people enjoying the sunshine. The trees were covered with leaves; the flowers were all in bloom; **every now and then** a bird sang. It was a lovely day.

Professor Allen was **about to** begin the second chapter

of his book when a man said, "Well, hello. The last time I saw you was in Philadelphia, wasn't it? Remember? But what are you doing here? Do you live in this town? I'm here to **see about something** for my office. I've been **up to my ears** in work."

"Why, I—" At first Herbert didn't know what to say. He hadn't been in Philadelphia since 1952, when he went there with his wife to visit her cousins. The man was mistaken, **to say the least.** Herbert had never seen him before.

The businessman must have noticed the strange expression on Herbert's face. **"What's the matter?"** he asked. "Don't you remember me?"

"Are you one of my wife's cousins?"

It was the other man's turn to have a strange expression. "I . . . I don't think so."

"Then I don't know you," the professor replied calmly. "The only people I know in Philadelphia are my wife's relatives."

"Excuse me," the businessman said. "I obviously made a mistake."

"That's all right," replied the professor and returned to his book. He had read only five minutes when, **all of a sudden,** a lady with a little boy spoke to him. "Pardon me, sir," said the lady. "You look like a kind person. Will you **keep an eye on** my little boy while I go across the street to the drugstore? I'll be back in five minutes."

Before he could say anything, the woman was gone. The professor put his book down and looked at the child. The child looked at the professor. "What's your name?" asked the boy.

"Herbert Allen. What's yours?"

"Allen Herbert."

"Really? That's very interesting." The professor thought about this coincidence for several minutes.

"I want some ice cream," the boy said, pointing to a man selling it nearby.

"All right," said the professor. "Come with me." He took the boy to the ice-cream man. "What flavor?" he asked the boy.

"Chocolate."

The professor did not notice that the boy was wearing a white shirt. Almost immediately there were spots of chocolate on it.

"Oh! Look at him!" cried the child's mother when she returned. "You're **to blame** for it! Why did you let him have it?"

"He wanted it," Professor Allen said timidly.

"He could have **done without** it!"

"I'm not used to being around children," the professor confessed.

"That's obvious," said the woman. "What am I going to do? I have to meet my mother-in-law here in ten minutes. If she sees Allen like this, she'll tell my husband I'm a careless housewife, **not to mention** a poor mother. I'll just have to take him home and change his shirt. I can't **get rid of** those spots here. I should have known **all along** not to leave Allen with a stranger." She hurried away angrily, pulling the chocolate-covered boy after her.

"That was **a close call**," Herbert told himself. "I thought for a minute she was going to have me arrested."

Once again Professor Allen opened his book. It was extremely interesting. **For the time being** he was able to forget the woman and her little boy.

Just fifteen minutes later someone touched his arm and asked, "Can you let me have a quarter, mister? **I'm broke** and I haven't had anything to eat all morning. **I've had my heart set on** a nice big hamburger all day. It's all I think about."

The professor, his mind deep in thought on a statement

by Voltaire, did not understand. "What did you say? You broke something?"

"No, no!" the man answered. "I said **I'm broke.** I need twenty-five cents for a hamburger."

The professor looked in his pockets. Finally he shook his head. "I'm sorry," he said, "but I don't have a quarter. Can you **make a fifty-cent piece do?**

The poor man looked at the professor as though he couldn't believe him. "I . . . I suppose so," he replied. He took the fifty-cent piece and, thanking the Professor, hurried away, shaking his head.

For the next half hour, nobody interrupted Professor Allen. However, he didn't read his book. There was too much to see: a big fire in the store down the street, an automobile accident at the corner, and a military parade that marched right in front of the park. In fact, all these things happened at the same time. It **goes without saying** that he had no time to read.

At 4:30 P.M. his alarm wristwatch notified him that **he'd better** go home. Two years before, his wife had given him the watch; before that he was always late for dinner. The professor got up from the bench in the park and started home.

When he reached the house, his wife opened the door for him. "Where have you been?" she asked, "and **what have you been up to?**" She seemed slightly annoyed. "The president of the Philosophical Society telephoned. The meeting tonight has been cancelled. I tried to reach you at the university, but you had already left."

"I had? Oh! Yes. Now I remember. It was such a fine afternoon that I went to the park."

His wife's attitude suddenly changed. "You did? I'm very glad, Herbert. The fresh air and sunshine **do you good.** You should go to the park every afternoon that the weather is nice."

"I can't go that often."

"Then go **every other** afternoon. You're too **hard on** yourself; always studying. Did you see anything interesting in the park?"

Professor Allen smiled. Today he would have lots of things to tell his wife.

"I know, I know," Mrs. Allen went on before he could speak. "As usual, you didn't see anything. Sometimes, Herbert, I wish you'd take your nose out of your books long enough to look at the world around you. Frankly, it's a lot more interesting."

Her husband nodded quietly, then went into the living room and sat down. He didn't **feel up to** arguing with her. And besides, maybe his wife was right. She almost always was. Maybe nothing really had happened in the park that afternoon. Perhaps he had gone to sleep and really just dreamed it all. Yet it had been so exciting that he'd **just as soon** believe it was true. He felt rather regretful. He was so absentminded that he couldn't trust his own ability to remember anything, not even something that happened an hour before!

Herbert was **about to** remove his coat when he saw a spot on his sleeve. Chocolate ice cream! He smiled. It hadn't been a dream after all. Everything had really happened. He got up from his chair and hurried into the kitchen to tell his wife.


## QUESTIONS ABOUT THE READING

1. Why did Professor Allen go to the park?
2. Who was the first person he met in the park?
3. What was his experience with Allen Herbert?
4. Why did he give the poor man fifty cents?

5. What made Professor Allen go home at 4:30?
6. What message did his wife give him when he got home?
7. What did he answer when his wife asked what had happened in the park?
8. What helped the professor remember his afternoon in the park?
9. Are you ever absentminded?
10. Do you think Professor Allen went to the park again? Why?

# UNIT II

## DRILL 6

### DIALOGUE

A: Friday is a holiday. Let's **take advantage of** the long weekend. Do you want to go to New York? We could leave Thursday night.

B: Okay. But **I'd rather** go on Friday. I have to get my car fixed.

A: All right. We can **take turns** driving.

B: Fine. We won't get so tired that way.

A: I'm **looking forward to** seeing New York. I've never been there.

B: I haven't either. Let's **make the most of** our weekend.

A: We can go sightseeing during the day. In the evening we can go to a play. Do you think we can get tickets?

B: I don't think we **stand a chance.** It's hard to get tickets on weekends. Anyway, we can try.

### DEFINITIONS

**take advantage of something**   to use something for one's own benefit

*Let's take advantage of this wonderful weather and go to the seashore.*

**would rather ('d rather)**   prefer
*Would you like pancakes for breakfast?*
*No, thank you. I'd rather have bacon and eggs.*

**take turns**   do something alternately with other persons
*There was only one dictionary, so the students had to take turns using it.*

**look forward to something**   anticipate with pleasure
*I've been working hard; I look forward to my vacation this year.*

**make the most of something**   do the best one can in a situation; get as much as possible out of it
*You made the most of your three days in Paris. I think you saw everything there.*

**stand a chance**   have the possibility
*Phillip wants a scholarship to Harvard but he doesn't stand a chance of getting one.*

## SUBSTITUTION DRILL

*Repeat the following sentences, using the substitutions listed.*

1.   Let's take advantage of the long weekend.
                 our free time.
                 John's offer.
                 this fine weather.
                 Betty's invitation.
                 Dave's good nature.
                 our opportunities.

2.   I'd rather go on Friday.
               see them tomorrow.

visit her this evening.
play golf on Saturday.
buy a bigger house.
find a newer car.
do it myself.

3. We can take turns driving.
using the dictionary.
reading the magazine.
dancing with Madge.
playing the piano.
cutting the grass.
using the camera.

4. I'm looking forward to seeing New York.
going with you.
visiting with them.
fishing in that lake.
dancing with Eleanor.
swimming in the ocean.
attending that exhibit.

5. Let's make the most of our weekend.
the sunny weather.
the time we have left.
our vacation.
Jim's invitation.
our day in the mountains.
our good fortune.

6. We don't stand a chance of getting tickets.
going with them.
finding our dog.
learning her name.
selling the car.
arriving on time.
borrowing the money.

## HOMEWORK EXERCISE

*Write a short dialogue with some of the following idioms:*

| | |
|---|---|
| take advantage of | look forward to |
| would rather | make the most of |
| take turns | stand a chance |

# DRILL 7

## DIALOGUE

A: I'm very proud of my daughter. She has quite a good memory. She **does her best** to remember all she reads. And she's only nine years old.

B: That's very good. Whom does she **take after?** You or your wife?

A: My wife. As a child Julia learned lots of poems **by heart.** She still knows **quite a few** of them.

B: I never could memorize poetry. **On the other hand,** I remember numbers. I never forget an address or a date.

A: Not even your wife's birthday?

B: Never! Alice would **take a dim view of** that!

## DEFINITIONS

**do one's best**   make the greatest effort that one can
> *I'm not sure I can be there tonight, but I'll **do my best**. It all depends on how much work I finish this afternoon.*

**take after someone**   resemble in appearance, personality, or character
> *Peter **takes after** his mother in personality and his father in appearance.*

26

**by heart**  by memorizing

*In elementary school I learned several of Longfellow's poems by heart.*

**quite a few**  many

*I haven't any recordings by Tom Jones, but I have quite a few by the Beatles.*

**on the other hand**  looking at the other side of the question

*Bert is extremely intelligent; on the other hand, he's a very lazy student.*

**take a dim view of something**  have a poor opinion of something; disapprove of something

*Mrs. Wright takes a dim view of the way her sister is raising her family.*


## SUBSTITUTION DRILL

*Repeat the following sentences, using the substitutions listed.*

1.   She does her best to remember everything.

please her parents.

learn her lessons.

be polite to them.

understand the language.

do her work well.

pronounce the words perfectly.

2.   Does she take after your wife?

her mother?

you?

your husband?

her father?

her uncle?

Mary?

3.  Julia learned many poems by heart.
    Bill learned many jokes
    Jimmy learned the grammar rules
    I'm learning square roots
    She has learned these idioms
    We're learning that story
    He learned those facts
4.  She knows quite a few poems.
         remembers
         understands
         recites
         likes
         reads
         writes
5.  I forget names. On the other hand, I remember numbers.
                faces.
                dates.
                addresses.
                voices.
                movie titles.
                recipes.
6.  Alice takes a dim view of my hobby.
                      your study habits.
                      John's driving.
                      Mary's cooking.
                      our vacation plans.
                      Bill's stories.
                      Jane's dresses.

## HOMEWORK EXERCISE

*Write an original paragraph, using at least three of the idioms you learned in this lesson.*

# DRILL 8

## DIALOGUE

A: I'm furious with Norma! She's always late.

B: Always? Why don't you **talk it over** with her? Encourage her to be **on time.**

A: Look! I've talked **till I'm blue in the face.** It's **out of the question.**

B: There must be something you can do.

A: I doubt it. Last night we went to a concert. Do you know what time we got there? Just **in time** to go out for the intermission!

B: I guess you're just **wasting your breath** then. Time means nothing to Norma.

## DEFINITIONS

**talk something over**   discuss
   *Jim always **talks things over** with his parents before he makes an important decision.*

**on time**   at the hour designated; not before or after that hour
   *Bill's very punctual; he's always **on time** for everything.*

**till one is blue in the face**   until one can say no more in trying to convince someone of something
   *Bob's father talked to him till **he was blue in the face,** but it did no good; the boy quit school anyway.*

**in time to**   be at a place at the right time to do something
   *George couldn't come for dinner, but he arrived **in time to** have dessert and coffee with us.*

**out of the question**   impossible; beyond consideration
>   *Your suggestion that we go swimming is **out of the question***; *it's much too cold today.*

**waste one's breath**   speak uselessly, to no purpose
>   *If you tell Jeff not to go, you'll just be **wasting your breath***; *he'll go anyway.*


## SUBSTITUTION DRILL

*Repeat the following sentences, using the substitutions listed.*

1.   Why don't you talk it over with her?
>>>       the project over with John?
>>>       your problem over with Professor Jones?
>>>       your plans over with your parents?
>>>       this idea over with the president?
>>>       everything over with them?
>>>       this case over with a lawyer?

2.   Encourage her to be on time.
>       Tell them to be
>       Be sure the boys are
>       I always try to be
>       He never gets here
>       Tell him he has to be
>       Ask them to try to be

3.   I've talked till I'm blue in the face.
>       He's argued till he's
>       She's explained till she's
>       We've repeated it till we're
>       They're discussed it till they're
>       I've gone over it till I'm
>       He's talked till he's

4.  Being late is out of the question.
    Selling the house
    Going to such a place
    Staying here
    Going with them
    Swimming in this weather
    Buying a new car
5.  We arrived in time to go out for intermission.
            have dinner with them.
            hear Jim's speech.
            talk to the Smiths.
            get a copy of the book.
            see the TV show.
            eat lunch.
6.  You're wasting your breath talking to him.
            explaining it.
            describing them.
            discussing it.
            giving the details.
            yelling at them.

## HOMEWORK EXERCISE

*Answer these questions, using idioms where possible.*

1.  Do you think a husband should discuss his problems with his wife?
2.  Are you always punctual for class?
3.  Do you know people whom it is useless to try to convince of anything?
4.  As long as a student's questions are reasonable, do you think the teacher should answer them?
5.  If you are invited to dinner, when should you arrive?
6.  How would you describe the way Charles talked to Bill?

He talked to Bill for three hours and tried to convince him not to go to New York at this time, but Bill refused to accept his idea.

# DRILL 9

## DIALOGUE

A:  What's wrong with you? Your face is swollen.

B:  My jaw aches. I don't know why.

A:  Let me see. **No wonder** it hurts! One of your teeth looks decayed. You'd better see a dentist **right away.**

B:  Do you think so? I've been **putting it off.** To tell the honest truth, dentists scare me. I **get cold feet** when I have to go to one.

A:  Don't be foolish. You'd **be better off** seeing one. I'll make an appointment for you.

B:  Okay. I **might as well** go. But find me one who doesn't hurt!

## DEFINITIONS

**no wonder**   it isn't surprising
*No wonder you're tired! You walked ten miles today!*

**right away**   immediately
*I'm sorry I forgot to get that medicine for you; I'll take care of it **right away**.*

**put something off**   postpone
*Because of the weather, we had to **put our picnic off** until next Sunday.*

**get cold feet**   become very cautious; be afraid to do something

> *John wanted to ask Vera to marry him, but **he got cold feet.***

**be better off**   be better on a long-term basis

> *Do you think I'd **be better off** quitting my present job and going to New York?*

**might as well**   it is a good idea (to do something), although not of major importance

> *If you're going to the library, I **might as well** go with you and return these books.*


## SUBSTITUTION DRILL

*Repeat the following sentences, using the substitutions listed.*

1.   No wonder your face is swollen!

> John's angry with you!
> Mary is late today!
> Fred isn't speaking to her!
> Bill wanted to leave early!
> Helen asked Bob to pay her!
> you lost your pocketbook!

2.   You'd better see a dentist right away.

> I'll take care of that
> She's coming to talk to us
> He wants to see her
> They need the money
> We ought to get it
> I have to see you

3.   I've been putting off going to the dentist.

> studying for my exam.
> paying my income tax.

writing a letter to Tom.

sending you that book.

asking her for the money.

telling her the truth.

4. I get cold feet when I have to go to the dentist.

give a talk.

ask for money.

see the doctor.

talk to Alice.

speak to my boss.

take medicine.

5. You'd be better off seeing a dentist.

going on a diet.

doing your homework.

telling her what happened.

leaving before it gets dark.

taking the children home now.

returning the book to the library.

6. I might as well go now.

study now.

speak to them.

telephone Bill.

go back to Miami.

tell the truth.

give her my answer.

## HOMEWORK EXERCISE

*Answer* TRUE *or* FALSE *to the following sentences, and correct those that are false.*

1. No wonder Jim is happy! He just lost a hundred dollars.
2. If you want me to do this work right away, I'll be glad to. I'll do it next month.

3.  If you are in a hurry to finish something, you shouldn't put it off.
4.  Jack wanted to marry Ella, so he got cold feet and asked her.
5.  I might as well go to the drugstore with you; I need some toothpaste.
6.  If Bob wants a good job, he'd be better off not to finish his education.

# DRILL 10

## DIALOGUE

A:  Your sales department is quite impressive. I see Bill White is **in charge of it.** He's a friend of mine.

B:  Bill is a fine worker. He's done very well here. **Little by little** sales have increased. Thanks to Bill White.

A:  Everyone likes Bill. He **makes friends** easily. That should be quite useful to you.

B:  Yes, it is. He's **hit upon** a new sales method, too. It's very effective. Tell me, where did you meet Bill?

A:  In high school. Even then he **showed promise.**

B:  We're lucky to have Bill with us. We need more like him: men who can **hold their own** in any situation.

## DEFINITIONS

**in charge of something**  responsible for something, such as the department of a large company or an activity for which arrangements must be made

> *Alex is **in charge of** the publicity committee for the school dance.*

35

**little by little**   gradually

*Frank broke his leg and couldn't walk for a long time, but **little by little** he began to use it again.*

**make friends**   form friendships with people

*Alice is very lonely, and I think her problem is that she doesn't know how to **make friends**.*

**hit upon something**   to discover something that will help make progress in a certain cause or situation

*The scientist worked for a long time but could not solve his problem; then, after many hours, he **hit upon** the right solution.*

**show promise**   give the impression of having the ability to do something in the future

*Betty has a beautiful voice and **shows promise** of being a great singer.*

**hold one's own**   to maintain oneself in, be equal to, a given situation

*Bob's parents don't worry about him; they know he can **hold his own** in his university studies.*


SUBSTITUTION DRILL

*Repeat the following sentences, using the substitution listed.*

1.   Bill White is in charge of the sales department.

                              meeting.

                              picnic plans.

                              office.

                              excursion.

                              party arrangements.

                              tour of the city.

2.   Little by little sales have increased.

                              he's learned English.

she's lost weight.

John's stopped smoking.

they paid for their car.

he lost interest in golf.

we saved enough money for the house.

3.     Bill makes friends easily. Everyone likes him.

George

Frank

Henry

John

Ed

Jack

4.     He's hit upon a new sales method.

a very good approach.

some interesting ideas.

an excellent method.

an exciting plan.

some new theories.

something revolutionary.

5.     Even then Bill showed promise.

As a boy

When he was young,

Long ago

When he began work,

Before he was twenty,

Until he got that job,

6.     We need men who can hold their own in any situation.

The company wants

There's always a demand for

I prefer

They hire

There are jobs for

The world can use more

## HOMEWORK EXERCISE

*Answer the following questions:*

1. If I do something little by little, do I work rapidly or slowly?
2. Is a person in charge responsible for something or only helping with it?
3. Does a person who makes friends easily usually have many friends or only a few?
4. Is it a compliment to say that someone shows promise?
5. Have you ever hit upon a good idea? Tell about it.
6. Can you hold your own in any situation?

# READING II

## THE VARIETY SHOW

"What our club needs is more members," the secretary reported.

"And membership dues," added the treasurer.

"How can we get them?" asked the vice-president.

"It's simple. We find a way to make people want to join the club," answered the president.

The International Friendship Club wasn't old, but it wasn't new, either. It had been organized two years before so that people from different countries could **make friends** with each other. At first there had been lots of activity, but **little by little** the club had become inactive. Now there was a possibility it might cease to exist if something wasn't done soon. A special meeting of the officers of the club was being held to **talk the situation over.** Something had to be done to improve the Club. They **took turns** making suggestions.

The meeting had started **on time,** promptly at eight o'clock, and finally at midnight it was decided that the best way to increase membership was to give a variety show with everyone participating. There was a lot of talent in the club, and they wanted to **take advantage of it.** It was hoped that people seeing the show would like to join an organization that could present entertaining programs. One or two members **took a dim view** of the idea, but they were outnumbered.

**Quite a few** different countries were represented in the club, and the possibilities for an enjoyable show were excellent. A committee was appointed, with Bill Harris **in charge of** it. Preparations began immediately.

Unfortunately, Bill had problems **right away.** When he asked members to participate in the show, they each replied, **"I'd rather** not be in it, but I'll **do my best** to help in other ways."

"Surely you can do something," Bill said to each person who refused to be in the show. "You can sing or dance or recite poetry."

"Not I," was the reply. "You're just **wasting your breath** asking."

It seemed to be **out of the question.** No one would be in the program. They all said they **got cold feet** every time they had to stand up in front of a crowd.

When Bill reported back to the committee, one member suggested. "We could do some tableaux; you know, present famous scenes from history, something like that. No one has to speak or move." The other committee members said no, the programs should be more modern, that no one did tableaux any more.

Bill was very discouraged. That evening, talking with his wife, Marilyn, he said, "When I tell the members what I want them to do they immediately say no. I talked to Mike Donaldson **till I was blue in the face,** but he still refused. **On the other hand,** he insisted he wanted to help." Bill shook his head. "Everyone wants to help but not in the one way I really need help! I think we'll just have to change our plans. Perhaps we'd **be better off** to postpone the show until later."

Marilyn did not reply **right away.** She sat thinking for a long time.

"I'm going to bed," Bill sighed wearily.

"Just a minute," Marilyn told him. "I have an idea. I think I know a way to **make the most of this situation**. Maybe you won't have to **put off** the show."

Bill, halfway up the stairs, looked doubtful as he stopped and faced his wife. There was a questioning expression on his face.

"Remember the Matsons?" Marilyn asked.

"Tim and Ellen Matson?"

"That's right. Remember that last year they gave a puppet show at the high school?"

Bill came back down the stairs. "Oh, yes. They were very good, as I recall. The show was terrific. Everyone enjoyed it."

"They made a lot of money for the school library, too."

"But I don't understand. What has a puppet show in the high school to do with the International Friendship Club? The Matsons give shows for children."

"Just be quiet and listen to my plan."

In a very short time, Marilyn explained her idea to Bill. When she finished, he nodded his head thoughtfully. "We **might as well** try it," he agreed. "Nothing lost, and it just might work."

"Of course it will work," Marilyn assured him. She went to the telephone and began to dial the Matsons' number.

Bill smiled at his wife. She was very confident. He decided she could **hold her own** in any situation. "Maybe you've **hit upon something**, Marilyn," he confessed. "It **shows real promise.**"

During the next month Bill Harris and his committee worked hard. They had not realized there was so much to do in preparation for such a program. One good thing, however, was that the performers did not have to learn anything **by heart.** Cooperation from the members, now that Marilyn had

41

given them a new idea, was excellent. In fact, so many people agreed to be in the show that they had to make a selection of the best acts.

Publicity for the show was very good, and on the evening of the performance, the auditorium was filled. Everyone was **looking forward to** the program. It was advertised as a puppet show that was different, with something for everyone from six to sixty.

"I'm not sure," Bill told Marilyn excitedly, taking his seat just **in time** to hear the overture, "but I think we **stand a chance** of making a lot of money for the club tonight. Quite a few people want to be members, too."

"Shh!" Marilyn whispered. "The curtain is going up. The show is going to begin."

A piano began to play and the curtain went up. A puppet dressed as a master of ceremonies announced the first number. A pretty girl puppet appeared. A feminine voice began to sing a humorous song about the difficulties of learning a foreign language. Whoever it was had a beautiful soprano voice, and the audience demanded an encore. "Doesn't that sound like Norah Lawton?" one member whispered to her husband. "I had no idea she could sing. But then her mother had a lovely voice; I guess Norah **takes after her**."

From the first act to the last one, the entire program was excellent. **No wonder** almost every performer had to repeat his or her number.

This had been Marilyn's idea. If the members refused to take part in the variety program because they didn't like to appear before big crowds, then a way would be found to avoid that. The puppet show had been the perfect solution!

## QUESTIONS ABOUT THE READING

1. What two things did the International Friendship Club need?
2. What was the purpose of the special meeting? How long did it last?
3. What decision was finally reached?
4. Did Bill Harris get help for the program? What was his problem?
5. Who helped Bill solve his problem?
6. Why wasn't it necessary for the performers to learn their parts in the program by heart?
7. Was the variety show a success?
8. Why had Marilyn's idea been a good one?
9. Do you belong to any clubs?
10. Do you like to participate in programs?

# UNIT III

## DRILL 11

### DIALOGUE

A: What a car! Every day it gets worse. Now it won't start **at all.** I guess I need a new one.

B: Here's an ad about a big auto sale. There are several good bargains. Do you want to look at it?

A: **By all means!** Let me see it. In my **frame of mind,** I'd buy a car today.

B: You can save a lot by paying cash.

A: Yes, I know. But remember, I'm a student. I have to **cut corners** where I can. I'll have to buy it **on credit.**

B: Well, be careful of the salesmen. Don't let them **put anything over on you.**

### DEFINITIONS

**at all**   used with negative expressions to give emphasis.
*I've read that book, but I didn't like it **at all.***

**by all means**   definitely, certainly
*When Mary asked her husband if he wanted steak for dinner, he replied, "**By all means!**"*

44

**frame of mind**  mental state

> *Be sure, Edith, that your husband is in a good **frame of mind** before you show him your new hat.*

**cut corners**  economize

> *When you have six children, you have to learn how to **cut corners**.*

**on credit**  make regular payments; not pay cash for a purchase

> *If you buy your car **on credit**, it's more expensive than if you pay cash.*

**put something over on someone**  deceive someone

> *I believed everything he said and then discovered none of it was true. He really **put something over on me**.*


## SUBSTITUTION DRILL

*Repeat the following sentences, using the substitutions listed.*

1.  My car won't start at all.
    This engine won't go
    My son won't eat
    That dog doesn't bark
    She won't speak to me
    They don't like fish
    He doesn't speak French

2.  By all means! Show me the newspaper.
    Tell me what I should do.
    Come with me to buy a car.
    Send me that information.
    Invite us to your wedding.
    Let us help you plan the picnic.
    Take my car if you want to.

3. In my frame of mind, I'd buy a car today
                        quit school right now.
                        go right over there.
                        tell him what I think.
                        refuse to do it.
                        say the wrong thing.
                        probably hit him.

4. Jim has to cut corners where he can.
   Alfred
   Paul
   Bert
   William
   Charles
   Alex

5. I'll have to buy it on credit.
   You can purchase it
   They buy everything
   We bought our house
   She bought her coat
   They'll buy their car
   I got my furniture

6. Don't let them put anything over on you.
                        her
                        Jim
                        the salesman
                        Alice
                        those people
                        that boy


## HOMEWORK EXERCISE

*Read the dialogue, filling in the blanks with the appropriate idiom.*

46

A: Have you had any news from your family?

B: No, I haven't heard anything_____. My father's supposed to send me some money. Could I borrow some from you if he doesn't send it soon?

A: _____. You know you can.

B: Thank you. I hate to borrow, but I'm worried about paying my room and board.

A: You can economize in some places, but that's one where it's impossible to_____.

B: I need a pair of shoes too, but in my present_____ _____, I don't want to spend the money.

A: You could buy them _____, but of course they cost more that way.

# DRILL 12

DIALOGUE

A: Have you heard from your brother recently?

B: Tom? No, I haven't. He must be furious with me. I've owed him a letter for six weeks. You know how it is: if you don't write letters, you don't get any. That **stands to reason.**

A: Don't blame yourself. Remember how busy you've been lately. For one thing, you've had exams all month.

B: That's true. But it's no excuse. **I've no business** neglecting my own brother.

A: Well, **never mind.** I'll write Tom a letter this evening. If you like, I can **put in a word for** you. Then you'll be **in the clear.**

B: Thanks a lot. I'll write a letter next week and **make up for** it.

# DEFINITIONS

**stand to reason**    be a logical conclusion
> *If he lied to you about one thing, it **stands to reason** that he'd lie about other things, too.*

**have no business doing something**    have no right to do something
> *You **had no business** using my car without asking me first!*

**never mind**    don't worry
> *If you can't get that book for me at the library, **never mind**. I'm going tomorrow, and I can get it then.*

**put in a word for someone, something**    say something positive for someone or something
> *If you have a chance to **put in a word** for me when you speak to the mayor, I'll appreciate it.*

**in the clear**    free from suspicion, blame, or obligation
> *The suspect's explanation to the police of why he was present at the scene of the crime was a very good one and put him **in the clear**.*

**make up for something**    compensate for something, often an unkind or inconsiderate act
> *Jim took my whole evening asking me questions about his physics exam. However, he **made up for** it the next afternoon by repairing my car.*


# SUBSTITUTION DRILL

*Repeat the following sentences, using the substitutions listed.*

1.    If you don't write letters, you won't receive any. That stands to reason.

If you don't study, you won't learn.

People are nice to us if we are nice to them.

Girls like boys who are polite to them.

Practising your English will improve it.

If we want to lose weight, we have to eat less.

It isn't healthy to stay up late every night.

2. STUDENT 1: Mary forgot to write to Tom. STUDENT 2: Never mind. She can do it tomorrow.

Bill didn't mail your card.

Alice forgot to phone Bill.

You didn't tell Mary the news.

We forgot to invite Jane.

I didn't wash my shirt.

Jack and Bob didn't do their homework.

3. I've no business neglecting my family.

leaving the children alone.

going to the movies tonight.

buying a new car right now.

taking time out for lunch today.

telling Anne all the details.

going fishing today.

4. I'll be glad to put in a word for you.

your idea.

Alex.

the Browns.

Bill's promotion.

Laura.

a new desk for Joe.

5. Pay the bill. Then you'll be in the clear.

Sign the contract.

Send the letter.

Return the papers.

Buy Ruth some flowers.

Call her immediately.

Tell them the truth.

6. I'll write a letter next week and make up for it.

I'll work an extra hour

I'll do something for them to

I'll send you five dollars to

I'll take them in my car

I'll study until midnight

I'll buy her some roses to

## HOMEWORK EXERCISE

*Change the following sentences into questions; then answer them in the negative.*

1. What that man said put him in the clear.
2. Mr. Brown promised to put in a word for me at the office.
3. I'll make up for your help with my homework by cutting your grass.
4. It stands to reason that if you break the law, you will be punished.

# DRILL 13

## DIALOGUE

A: It's a beautiful day. Let's go for a walk.

B: I'd like to, but I feel **under the weather**. I think I'm **catching cold**.

A: That's too bad. You'd better **watch your step** then. A cold is no fun.

B: I guess it **serves me right.** I went out without a coat last night. Anyway, I'll stay in the house and rest today.

A: The best cure for a cold is to **take it easy.** Drink lots of liquids, too.

B. I'll do that. I don't want to **go from bad to worse.** I might catch the flu.


## DEFINITIONS

**under the weather**   not feeling well physically
*I'm feeling a little **under the weather** tonight, so I think I'll go to bed early.*

**catch cold**   to get a cold
*I enjoyed the football game, but it was such a wet, windy day that I **caught cold**.*

**watch one's step**   be careful in one's conduct
***Watch your step**, young man! If you're late for work again, you'll lose your job.*

**serve someone right**   get what someone deserves (usually used in the negative sense)
*It **serves Albert right** that he missed the train. Maybe he'll learn to be on time after this.*

**take it easy**   relax
*Steve, you're working too hard. Sit down and **take it easy** for a while.*

**go from bad to worse**   become progressively worse
*After Joe became president of the club, we thought everything would be all right. Instead, things went **from bad to worse**.*

## SUBSTITUTION DRILL

*Repeat the following sentences, using the substitutions listed.*

1. I feel a little under the weather today.
   He feels
   Mary feels
   They feel
   We feel
   John feels
   My mother feels

2. I think I'm catching cold.
   Jim believes he's
   Alice feels she's
   My aunt thinks she's
   Bob doesn't believe he's
   Frank says he's
   Mother denies she's

3. You'd better watch your step, Tom!
   You should
   You ought to
   You must
   You have to
   I told you to
   You've got to

4. It serves me right if I catch cold.
   am late for class.
   miss my train.
   lose my job.
   catch pneumonia.
   don't get the position.
   don't find my wallet.

5. For a cold, the best cure is to take it easy.
   For your nerves you should learn to

If you want to enjoy life, you ought to

If you want people to like you, you must

One lesson Tom had to learn was to

My father is healthy because he knows how to

The reason I feel well is that I've learned to

6.  I don't want to go from bad to worse.

That situation will go

Their relationship has gone

Her studies have gone

The condition of this house has gone

Our relations with that country have gone

His work for the company has gone

## HOMEWORK EXERCISE

*Rewrite the following paragraph, using idioms where it is possible to do so.*

Bob was not feeling very well. He seemed to be getting a cold. His mother told him to be careful or the cold would become worse; he might get influenza. She told him to relax and drink lots of liquid. "I guess I deserve this cold," Bob admitted. "I went out in the rain without a coat last night."

# DRILL 14

## DIALOGUE

A: **I put my foot in it** today.

B: What happened?

A: **I had words with** my aunt. I felt terrible about it later. But I'd been **on edge** all morning.

B: **Come to the point.** Why did you argue?

A: My son Billy misbehaved. I punished him. Aunt Rose defended Billy. That was **the last straw!** I told her not to interfere.

B: Is everything all right now?

A: Yes, everything is fine. I'm glad I **took a stand** with Aunt Rose, though. We understand each other better now.


## DEFINITIONS

**put one's foot in it**   say or do the wrong thing
> *Joe **put his foot in it** when he told Ethel she looked like Dora. The two girls dislike each other.*

**have words with someone**   quarrel; argue with some person
> *I **had words with** the manager of that store, because he refused to refund my money for a TV set that wasn't operating properly.*

**on edge**   nervous; irritable
> *What's the matter with Ray? He seems to be **on edge** about something.*

**come to the point**   be definite, precise in telling something
> *Professor Johnson's stories are interesting but long, and he never seems to **come to the point**.*

**the last straw**   the point beyond which one can endure no more
> *When I told him to pay me the money he owed me, he said he couldn't; instead he asked to borrow an additional five dollars. That was **the last straw!***

**take a stand on something**   make a firm decision about something
> *I don't like the way Tom operates. One day he says one thing and another day he says the opposite. I wish he'd **take a stand** on something.*

## SUBSTITUTION DRILL

*Repeat the following sentences, using the substitutions listed.*

1. Jim put his foot in it today. He argued with the teacher.
   He spoke back to his father.
   He had an accident with his brother's car.
   He told Alice she wasn't pretty.
   He lost Professor Smith's book.
   He told his mother-in-law she was wrong.
   He told his wife he didn't like her cooking.

2. I had words with my aunt today.
   Emily
   my wife
   Leonard
   Geraldine
   my boss
   Jim's brother

3. I've been on edge all morning.
   this afternoon.
   all day.
   for several days.
   since Mary left.
   lately.
   this week.

4. Come to the point. Why did you argue?
   Why are you late?
   Where is the money?
   Who took my car?

When will you bring it?

What time are you leaving?

Why can't you go?

5. Aunt Rose defended Billy. That was the last straw!

Jim wrecked my car.

He asked to borrow some money.

She ruined her stockings.

The boss wouldn't give him a raise.

At the last minute Ben couldn't pay.

I couldn't remember the answer.

6. I'm glad I took a stand with Aunt Rose.

my brother-in-law.

my co-worker.

the telephone company.

that salesman.

that government official.

those students.

## HOMEWORK EXERCISE

*Write a short composition about one of these situations:*

1. A time when you had words with someone
2. A time when you put your foot in it
3. A time when you felt like saying "That's the last straw!"

# DRILL 15

## DIALOGUE

A: Good afternoon. May I help you?

B: Thank you. I need some gloves for skiing. I've already been to three stores. **So far** I haven't found anything I like.

A: Perhaps this pair will **serve your purpose.**

B: These look good. **In fact,** they're the best ones I've seen yet. They're quite expensive, though. Frankly, I **draw the line** at spending much for gloves.

A: Are you in a hurry for them? Can you wait a few days?

B: I suppose so. But why?

A: We're having a sale. Next week these gloves will be half price. Why don't you wait?

B: **So much the better.** Of course I'll wait. Thanks for telling me.

A: **Think nothing of it.**


## DEFINITIONS

**so far**    until now

*I've been on a diet for two weeks, but* **so far** *I haven't lost any weight.*

**serve someone's purpose**    be useful to someone for a certain purpose

*I prefer cream for this recipe, but milk will* **serve my purpose.**

**in fact**    actually; really

*Yes, I know Robert Johnson.* **In fact,** *he's my cousin.*

**draw the line**    refuse to go beyond a certain point in doing something

*I'll pay for my wife's ticket to that lecture on modern art, but I* **draw the line** *at attending with her!*

**so much the better**    that's even better

*Jeanne is delighted to come to our party; if she insists on bringing a cake,* **so much the better.**

**Think nothing of it.**   forget it; don't worry about it; that's all right

> A:   *I'm sorry I forgot to bring your book.*
> B:   *That's all right.* **Think nothing of it.**


## SUBSTITUTION DRILL

*Repeat the following sentences, using the substitutions listed.*

1.   So far I haven't found anything I like.
>> he hasn't told us what happened.
>> she hasn't insisted on leaving.
>> they haven't explained it to us.
>> we haven't bought any of those.
>> Bill hasn't given me a present.
>> Ellen hasn't wanted to go with us.

2.   Perhaps this pair will serve your purpose.
> Maybe this shirt
> I think these gloves
> I believe that coat
> It's possible this hat
> I hope these buttons
> I doubt that this cap

3.   In fact, they're the best gloves I've seen yet.
>> these shoes are excellent.
>> he's a very good teacher.
>> Tom's the best worker we have.
>> she's my wife's sister.
>> I have that book right here.
>> he was a good friend of my father's.

4.   I draw the line at spending much money on a tie.
>>> going so far just to see a movie.
>>> accepting so much responsibility.
>>> taking all of them.

buying one of each kind.

preparing lunch for them.

telling a lie about it.

5.     If the gloves will be half price, so much the better.

If Jim can go there with us,

If you're used to studying hard,

If we have enough for everyone,

If they can pay for it with cash,

If Caroline wants to take care of it,

If Bob understands what needs to be done,

6.     STUDENT 1: Thanks for telling me. STUDENT 2: Think nothing of it.

I appreciate your help.

I'm grateful to you.

Thank you for the gift.

Thanks for the information.

We don't know how to thank you.

I appreciate all you've done for us.


## HOMEWORK EXERCISE

*Rearrange these groups of words to make correct sentences.*

| 1. | | 2. | | 3. | | 4. | |
|---|---|---|---|---|---|---|---|
| luck | | serve | | line | | better | |
| we've | | lamp | | much | | the | |
| far | | think | | I | | much | |
| good | | you | | at | | so | |
| had | | this | | money | | us | |
| so | | purpose | | spending | | with | |
| | | will | | draw | | go | |
| | | our | | the | | can | |
| | | do | | that | | Alice | |
| | | ? | | | | if | |

59

# READING III

## LESSON FOR A DOCTOR

Frank Burke got into his car and drove quickly down the street, away from the hospital. He'd just **had words with** one of the other doctors, and he was furious. Old Dr. MacDonald knew that the Wilkins boy was Frank's patient. He **had no business** interfering, none **at all**. Frank accepted a lot of criticism from the older physician, but he **drew the line** at this. Just because MacDonald was the oldest doctor at Mayfair Hospital, he thought he could do anything he wished; the younger men should **think nothing of it**. Anyone would think Dr. Burke was incapable of treating someone who had just **caught cold!**

The other doctors at Mayfair Hospital all had complaints about the older man. As one intern said, "He makes you feel you're trying to **put something over on someone** just because you want to be a doctor!"

Another thing, Dr. MacDonald's methods were extremely old-fashioned. He was, for example, quite unprofessional in his treatment of patients. It was true that he was very friendly toward them, but he spent too much time with each; other patients often had to wait hours to see him. His attitude towards the younger physicians was that of an intelligent, superior being dealing with a lot of idiots. Well, if the facts were known, young Dr. Burke, at 31, probably had twice the medical education that MacDonald had at 64! Frank had attended one of the best medical schools in the country; it **stood to reason** that he would become an excellent physician. One day, when the opportunity arose to do so, he'd **take a stand** with Dr. MacDonald, **come to the point,** tell him exactly what he thought of him. In his present **frame of mind,** that would be easy!

Frank glanced down and saw that the speedometer registered forty-five miles an hour, ten miles over the speed limit in this zone. "**Take it easy,**" he told himself. He was so much **on edge** thinking about Dr. MacDonald that he hadn't realized he was driving so fast. It was lucky there were no policemen around at the moment. All he needed was to be arrested for speeding while thinking about Dr. MacDonald! Maybe it would **serve him right,** but that would be **the last straw!**

This being his free afternoon, Frank decided to take a drive in the country. He had been extremely busy all morning, and now he needed to relax. **So far** it hadn't been a very good day for him.

Autumn was here, and the red and gold leaves of the trees had never been more spectacular. His anger began to leave him as he viewed the beautiful scenery.

After a while he came to a small town in a valley. He had driven through it many times but had never stopped. He decided to do so. At the edge of the town was a hospital. Why not visit it? He had plenty of time. For a doctor working in one of the state's largest, most modern hospitals, it would be interesting to see this small, old-fashioned one.

A very attractive nurse greeted him. "May I help you?" she asked pleasantly.

Frank told her who he was. "I just want to look around a little," he explained.

"Come in, **by all means**," she invited. "Dr. Bryant is free at the moment. He's been **under the weather** lately and hasn't been working so hard as usual. He's our director, and I'm sure he'll be pleased to talk with you."

Within five minutes Frank was being given a tour of the hospital by its director. "Not the most modern equipment in the world, but **never mind,** it **serves the purpose.** As you can imagine, we bought most of it **on credit,** and we had to **cut corners** even to do that."

When Dr. Bryant learned where Frank worked, he exclaimed enthusiastically, "Then of course you know my old friend, Ralph MacDonald!"

"Yes, I know Dr. MacDonald." Frank would have to **watch his step** with what he said, or he might **put his foot in it.** Dr. Bryant obviously respected MacDonald a great deal.

"A fine man and one of the best doctors in the country," he told Frank. "They don't seem to make doctors like him anymore—men who really dedicate their whole lives to medicine. You may be sure I **put in a word** for him and his way of practising medicine every time I have the chance."

Frank wanted to comment that there was a big difference between dedication and interference, but he said nothing. He hoped the other physician wouldn't ask **his** opinion of Dr. MacDonald. Today wasn't the day to ask such a thing.

"I worked with Ralph when I first came out of medical school," Dr. Bryant said. **"In fact,** I can say that I am head of this hospital today because of him. Working with Ralph MacDonald taught me the most important lesson I had to learn as a doctor."

Frank stared at Dr. Bryant questioningly. What could anyone learn from old Dr. MacDonald? Everyone knew that his methods were out-of-date.

"I learned," Dr. Bryant was saying, "that there are certain qualifications all doctors must have. In every medical school they make sure the students remember what they are. There is one, however, that they don't always tell us. We have to learn it for ourselves and some doctors never do. Ralph MacDonald taught me that one. I'll always be grateful to him for that.

"It wasn't anything he said, really. It was something I observed in him. He showed his patients that he cared about them. At the moment he was with them, it was as though there was no other patient in the world. They were more than just patients to Ralph; they were his friends. If he sometimes acted rather stern, **so much the better;** they understood that he meant it for their own good. The response sometimes was almost miraculous.

"I know that Ralph has been criticized. There are certain people, especially more modern-thinking physicians, who claim he doesn't have a very professional manner. That depends on what you call professional. I only know that his quality of caring for people and wanting to help them compensates for everything else. Now come this way, Dr. Burke. I want to show you our new operating room. We're quite proud of it."

Driving back to the city that afternoon, Frank thought over Dr. Bryant's observations. He suddenly realized he had been wrong about Dr. MacDonald. To that old physician at Mayfair Hospital, his patients were individuals who needed his understanding of their problems. They were more than just human bodies in need of remedy.

Thinking back on what had happened that morning, Frank knew now why Dr. MacDonald had interfered in the case of the little Wilkins boy. He had observed that Frank, in his very efficient, professional manner, was neglecting the most important thing of all: concern for the boy as a person. His efficiency could not be criticized, but neither could it put him **in the clear** with Dr. MacDonald if Frank couldn't communicate to Jimmy Wilkins that he cared about him.

When he reached the city, Frank drove directly to the hospital.

"Hi, Jimmy," he said as he entered the Wilkins boy's room. "How do you feel this evening?"

The boy looked surprised. "Hello," he replied, smiling. "I thought it was Dr. MacDonald. He's the only one who comes to see me in the evening."

"Well, Jimmy, you've going to see a lot more of me, too, from now on."

Just then Dr. MacDonald entered the room. He had an expression of astonishment, though not disapproval, on his face upon seeing Frank Burke there. "Well, you're here, are you?"

"Just checking up on my young friend," Frank replied.

"Well, it's about time. Keep it up and maybe you'll even be a good doctor some day."

Frank smiled. Yes, he thought, after today's lesson maybe he would be. At least he was going to try.

## QUESTIONS ABOUT THE READING

1.  Why did Dr. Burke get angry with Dr. MacDonald?
2.  Where was he driving?
3.  Where did he stop? Why?
4.  What did he decide to visit?
5.  Who took him on a tour of the hospital?
6.  Was it a modern hospital?
7.  What did the director of the hospital tell him about Dr. MacDonald?
8.  Where did Frank go next?
9.  What did Dr. MacDonald say when he saw Frank that evening?
10.  What was the lesson Frank learned that day?

64

# UNIT IV

## DRILL 16

### DIALOGUE

A:  How was your trip to Chicago?

B:  I wish I'd spent my vacation here.

A:  **In other words,** you didn't like Chicago.

B:  Oh, it wasn't that. I liked the city very much. But I got sick while I was there.

A:  I'm sorry to hear that.

B:  I **came near** having to call the doctor. But I had some medicine and I took that. I always carry it, just to **be on the safe side.**

A:  Lucky you had it **on hand.**

B:  **Little did I think** I'd get sick in Chicago. Next time I won't take chances. I'll make sure I'm in good health before I leave.

A:  **Keep your fingers crossed!**

### DEFINITIONS

**in other words**   to say something in a different way

*You say you're going to be late at the office?* ***In other words,*** *you'll be late for supper tonight.*

**come near (+ -ing form of verb)**   almost do something
> *I was so angry last night I **came near** telling George what I thought of him.*

**be on the safe side**   not to take any chances
> *I don't think it's going to rain today, but I'm going to take my umbrella, just **to be on the safe side**.*

**on hand**   available
> *Do you have any aspirin **on hand**? I have a terrible headache.*

**little does one think**   one cannot imagine
> *When Bill asked Helen to go to the dance with him, **little did he think** that she already had a date.*

**keep one's fingers crossed**   hope to have good results in an effort; hope that nothing will go wrong
> *I'm on my way to take my examinations. **Keep your fingers crossed** for me!*


## SUBSTITUTION DRILL

*Repeat the following sentences, using the substitutions listed.*

1.   In other words, you didn't like Chicago.
>             he isn't responsible for it.
>             they can't be here today.
>             she doesn't intend to go.
>             the Smiths don't want that house.
>             Frank hasn't had time to do it.
>             we aren't invited to go with them.

2.   I came near having to call the doctor.
>             buy a new car.

tell them to leave.
go to a dentist.
ask Tim for a dollar.
speak to him sharply.
take medicine for it.

3. I always carry an umbrella, just to be on the safe side.
   He always tells us where he's going,
   She pays them in advance,
   We keep our car in good condition,
   They check everything carefully,
   I take an extra key,
   Albert takes vitamins,

4. Little did I think I'd get sick.
   they'd be late.
   she'd get angry.
   we'd get lost.
   he'd go with us.
   you'd come early.
   I'd have trouble.

5. Lucky you had your medicine on hand.
   I always keep some aspirins
   They usually have coffee
   We don't often have tea
   He didn't have a copy
   She tries to keep stamps
   I never seem to have envelopes

6. I have an exam today. Keep your fingers crossed for me!
   I have to give a speech today.
   I'm taking my driving test this morning.
   I have an interview for a job this afternoon.
   I hope my car can make the trip to New York.
   I'm going to ask Brigit for a date tonight.
   I'm going to bet five dollars on that horse.

## HOMEWORK EXERCISE

*Fill in the blanks with the appropriate idiom.*

1.  You say you can't go tonight. _____, you really don't want to go. Isn't that the truth?
2.  Martha gave me her address but I didn't have a pencil _____, so I couldn't write it down.
3.  It's a good idea to keep your car in good condition, _____.
4.  I got very angry with Joe yesterday. I _____ hitting him.
5.  I'm going downtown now to see about a job. Please _____ for me!
6.  I didn't ask Bob to go with us. _____ he'd want to.

# DRILL 17

## DIALOGUE

A:  What's happened to Edith Jones? I've **lost track of** her lately.

B:  I don't know, and I really don't care. Edith always **rubbed me the wrong way.**

A:  Really? **I took it for granted** you two were good friends.

B:  We used to be. Not any more, though. I got tired of her remarks.

A:  I'm sorry to hear that. Edith's really a nice girl, though. And life's too short to stay angry at someone. Come on. **Let bygones be bygones.** I'm sure she'd like to be friends again. **Meet her halfway.**

B:  I suppose you're right. I'll **turn over a new leaf** and start again. It's no fun being mad at people.

# DEFINITIONS

**lose track of someone, something**   cease having information about; not be informed currently about someone or something

> *I've **lost track of** Mr. and Mrs. Brown. Where are they now?*

**rub someone the wrong way**   irritate

> *Henry isn't a very diplomatic person; he's always **rubbing people the wrong way**.*

**take something for granted**   assume, without giving it a thought, that something is a certain way

> *Excuse me for not introducing you to Bert. I **took it for granted** that you two knew each other.*

**let bygones be bygones**   forget and forgive unpleasant happenings in the past

> *I decided to **let bygones be bygones** and not say anything about the way Alice spoke to me last week.*

**meet someone halfway**   to compromise with someone in a situation where the opinions differ

> *Charles has very definite ideas but he's not unreasonable; he **tries to meet you halfway**.*

**turn over a new leaf**   make a fresh start

> *Every January first, many people **turn over a new leaf** and try to live better lives.*

## SUBSTITUTION DRILL

*Repeat the following sentences, using the substitutions listed.*

1.   I've lost track of Edith.
>      Bill.

George.
the Blacks.
Donald.
Larry.
Margaret.

2.    Edith rubs me the wrong way.
Marjorie
Frances
Oliver
Max
Professor Jones
Bert

3.    I took it for granted you were friends.
they were coming.
we were going.
she was absent.
he wanted that book.
you didn't have one.
it was on Tuesday.

4.    Why don't you let bygones be bygones?
Why doesn't Connie
Why can't Frank
Why don't they
Why couldn't she
Why doesn't Lucy
Why wouldn't he

5.    Meet her halfway.
John
them
us
Alice
Jack
Phyllis

70

6. I'll turn over a new leaf.
   You should
   They ought to
   Jim says he'll
   Mary promises to
   Bob has decided to
   Marian said she'd

## HOMEWORK EXERCISE

*Complete these sentences:*

1. If you'll meet me halfway, _____.
2. Where can I find the Whites? _____.
3. Why don't you forget what Alex said and _____?
4. Every January first, it's a good idea to _____.
5. What Bill said yesterday made me angry; it _____.
6. Jack didn't know we moved. He thought we still lived on Elm Street. He _____.

# DRILL 18

## DIALOGUE

A: Do you like to dance?

B: **As a rule** I do. But it depends on what you mean. I don't **go in for** the new dances.

A: Why not? I like them. They're **in keeping with** the times.

B: I guess I'm old-fashioned, then. **As far as I'm concerned,** they're terrible! Besides, I can't **tell them apart.** The new dances all look the same to me.

A: Come on. Give them another chance. Go with me to the school dance tonight. Be my guest.

B:  Well, all right. Maybe I'll like them better this time. But I insist we **go Dutch.** I'll be your guest next time.

## DEFINITIONS

**as a rule**   usually; customarily
> *As a rule I never stay out late on a week night, because I have to get up early the next morning.*

**(not) go in (much) for something** (used more in negative) like; have a strong interest in
> *I like golf, but I don't go in much for tennis.*

**be in keeping with something**   be appropriate
> *I liked what Professor Thomas said to the International Club, because his words were in keeping with the purpose of the Club.*

**as far as someone is concerned**   in one's opinion
> *As far as I'm concerned, it's too cold to go swimming this afternoon.*

**tell (two things) apart**   distinguish between two things
> *I know that one stone is a diamond and the other is only glass, but frankly I can't tell them apart.*

**go Dutch**   each person pay his own way to a movie, restaurant, etc.
> *Thanks for asking me to go to lunch with you, but I insist we go Dutch.*

## SUBSTITUTION DRILL

*Repeat the following sentences, using the substitutions listed.*

1.   As a rule I like to dance.
>       Jim doesn't eat lunch.

they don't go out in the evening.
we go to bed at ten o'clock.
I don't drive to work.
he likes cream in his coffee.
George walks to work.

2. I don't go in for the new dances.
card playing.
winter sports.
tennis.
hunting and fishing.
ping-pong.
bowling.

3. They're in keeping with the times.
his own ideas.
the lesson plan.
modern trends.
the twentieth century.
the president's beliefs.
Professor White's theories.

4. As far as I'm concerned, they're terrible.
he's a good writer.
she's a great actress.
we're making progress.
it's much too late to go.
he's completely wrong.
you have a fine plan.

5. I can't tell those dances apart.
the twins
those two boys
these coats
your aunts
their two cars
her paintings

6. We decided to go Dutch.

They
Bill and Jeanne
the two students
the group of teachers
June and Henry
The three girls


## HOMEWORK EXERCISE

*Write a brief paragraph on one of these subjects:*

1. Going Dutch
2. A sport I go in for
3. Modern dancing is in keeping with the times.


# DRILL 19

---

## DIALOGUE

A: Someone named Cooper phoned this afternoon. He **left word** for you to call him. He's at the Biltmore Hotel. You can **get in touch with** him there.

B: That's my old friend, Dave Cooper. I knew he was coming to town. I didn't expect him today, though. I must have **got mixed up** on the dates.

A: Shall we ask him to our party tonight?

B: I'd like to. But we've already invited fifty people. And the apartment is rather small.

A: Don't worry. We can always **make room for** one more.

B: That's true. And the other guests will like Dave. He's very friendly.

A:    Be sure to tell him not to **dress up**. It's an informal party, you know.

B:    Okay. I'll go get Dave in the car. He doesn't know this city. He might **lose his way** coming alone.


## DEFINITIONS

**leave word**    leave a message
> *Ralph had to go, but he **left word** that you should meet him at the hotel.*

**get in touch with someone**    communicate with someone by phone, telegraph, mail, etc.
> *I can't talk with you now, but I'll **get in touch with you** this evening by phone.*

**get mixed up**    become confused
> *Nancy has six children, and I always **get mixed up** on their names.*

**make room for something, someone**    allow space for; arrange space for
> *There were already three people on the sofa, but they moved over and **made room for** me to sit down.*

**dress up**    put on one's best clothes
> *When Celia **dresses up**, she is more beautiful than a movie actress.*

**lose one's way**    go in the wrong direction in trying to find a place and become lost
> *I'm sorry to be late, but **I lost my way**; I went east instead of west.*

# SUBSTITUTION DRILL

*Repeat the following sentences, using the substitutions listed.*

1.     Dave left word for you to call him.

                        go directly to Boston.

                        give Bill the money.

                        send him the book.

                        meet him at the theater.

                        sign these papers.

                        be at the office at eight o'clock.

2.     I got mixed up on the dates.

                        hour.

                        day of the week.

                        time.

                        place to meet.

                        directions.

                        best way to get here.

3.     You can get in touch with Dave at the hotel.

                                by phone.

                                at his office.

                                by telegram.

                                by letter.

                                tomorrow.

                                downtown.

4.     We can always make room for one more.

                            another person.

                            two more.

                            a few more.

                            an extra one or two.

                            you.

                            someone like Tina.

5.     Tell Dave not to dress up for the party.

                        the picnic.

the dance.

our dinner.

Mary's beach party.

the trip to the museum.

the day on the boat.

6. He might lose his way coming alone.

driving his car.

taking the bus.

going alone.

coming by himself.

not knowing the city.

being a stranger here.

## HOMEWORK EXERCISE

*Answer these questions:*

1. When was the last time you lost your way?
2. Do you like to dress up for a party?
3. Is it true that "we can always make room for one more"?
4. Are you a reliable person to leave word with?
5. Did you ever get mixed up on a date or place to meet?
6. Where can I get in touch with you?

# DRILL 20

## DIALOGUE

A: I have to send Paul a telegram. Do you know his address?

B: Just wire him **in care of** James Black, Austin, Texas. Why are you sending him a telegram?

A: When he left last night, he took my history book. I need it.

B: That's too bad. He didn't take it **on purpose,** did he?

A: I'm sure he didn't. Actually, it's my own fault. I didn't **pay attention** to what I was doing. I left it on the desk with his books.

B: How soon do you need it?

A: For Friday. I'm **taking part in** a panel discussion. It's about the War of 1812. My problem is this: I don't **know the first thing about** it.

B: Watch where you put your books **from now on.**

A: I will.


## DEFINITIONS

**in care of someone**   write to one person at the address of another person
> *When you write to Roy, be sure to put "in care of Mrs. John Briggs" on the envelope.*

**on purpose**   intentionally
> *Jimmy hit his little brother in the eye, but he didn't do it on purpose.*

**pay attention**   look at or listen to with concentration
> *Now children, pay attention; I'm going to tell you something very important.*

**take part in something**   participate in some activity
> *I enjoy seeing a play, but I've never taken part in one.*

**(not) know the first thing about something** (usually used in the negative)   have knowledge of
> *I don't know the first thing about an automobile engine.*

**from now on**   from this moment forward
> *I'm too fat. From now on I'm not going to eat so much.*

## SUBSTITUTION DRILL

*Repeat the following sentences, using the substitutions listed.*

1. Wire him in care of James Black, Austin, Texas.
   - William Brown, Toledo, Ohio.
   - Richard Gray, Miami, Florida.
   - John Washburn, Bangor, Maine.
   - Nancy O'Neill, Washington, D.C.
   - Robert Sheeler, Chicago, Illinois.
   - Ruben Hamby, Toledo, Ohio.

2. Paul didn't take it on purpose.
   - Jane didn't say that
   - We didn't do it
   - She wouldn't tell them
   - Sam wasn't absent
   - Harriet didn't keep it
   - Dick wouldn't say that

3. I didn't pay attention to what I was doing.
   - where I was going.
   - what I was saying.
   - what I was telling them.
   - what the teacher was saying.
   - what he said to us.
   - where they were taking me.

4. I'm taking part in a panel discussion.
   - a play.
   - a school program.
   - a committee meeting.
   - a tennis match.
   - a debate at school.
   - a piano recital.

5. I don't know the first thing about American History.
   - geopolitics.

physics.
American football.
atomic energy.
agronomy.
French literature.

6. Watch where you put your books from now on.
Be careful what you say
Try to be on time
Take better care of your health
Drive more carefully
Speak better English
Work harder

## HOMEWORK EXERCISE

*Write an original sentence for each of the idioms in this lesson.*

| | |
|---|---|
| in care of | take part in |
| on purpose | (not) know the first thing about |
| pay attention | from now on |

# READING IV

## THE RED BOWL

It would be fun, Alex thought, to give Cora something for no reason at all. He had not planned to give his wife a present, but when he saw the red glass fruit bowl, he could not resist it. It **came near** being the prettiest bowl he had ever seen. From time to time he bought Cora such a gift. She **went in for** beautiful dishes. He himself didn't **know the first thing** about them.

"I'll take this one," Alex told the clerk.

"Yes, sir. Would you like the individual fruit dishes that go with the bowl?"

Before he answered, Alex looked to see if he had enough money, **just to be on the safe side. As a rule** he didn't carry much with him. "Not today, thank you. Perhaps later."

"Very good, sir. We keep them **on hand** regularly. Do you want this wrapped as a gift?"

"Yes, please."

"What is the occasion? A birthday, perhaps?"

"No, no special occasion." That wasn't exactly true. Cora always made it an occasion when Alex brought her a gift.

In a few minutes he was on his way home.

They lived in a modest little house, and although it was rather old-fashioned, it was in a nice section of the city. It wasn't too far from the office where Alex worked. There was a bus stop at the corner, and two blocks away was a big shopping center where Cora could get almost anything she needed. **In other words,** it was in an excellent location. Alex and Cora Jackson liked their neighbors, too; they were all very friendly people. Both Alex and Cora **took part in** community activities. They were very happy there.

Alex had taken time from work and left the office at five o'clock this particular afternoon. He **had left word** with his secretary that if Cora telephoned to tell her he had gone downtown. "If there's anything urgent," he had said, "you **can get in touch with me** at Hartman's Department Store."

He wanted to get to Hartman's in time to buy a pair of shoes before the store closed at six P.M. Hartman's had the best shoe department in town.

It didn't take long to find a pair of shoes. There were two pairs that he liked, but one cost ten dollars more than the other pair. However, to Alex they looked the same. In fact, it was impossible to **tell them apart;** so he took the cheaper pair.

Instead of taking the elevator down to the main floor, Alex decided to walk. He wanted to stop on the second floor and look at some new fishing equipment in the sports department.

At the bottom of the stairs was the glassware department, and Alex had to pass through it to get to the fishing things. What a lot of pretty glass! Cora would love it!

That morning when he left the house to go to work, Alex had noticed that Cora seemed preoccupied. She hadn't been the usual happy wife who kissed him good-bye and sent him off to work in a wonderful mood every day. She was usually so sweet and cheerful that he **took it for granted** she would always be so. Today she had had very little to say. About the only thing she had done was to remind him to send a birthday card to his Uncle Frank. "And don't forget to send it **in care of** your cousin George," she said.

When Alex asked Cora if she felt all right, she replied, "Of course. I feel fine." But something was troubling her, he was sure. She seemed to be waiting for something, but he had no idea what it was. It didn't help any when she said, "Don't **lose your way** home tonight." What did she mean by such a statement? Well, he guessed he'd just have to expect her to have her good days and bad ones, like everyone else. He couldn't expect her to be in excellent spirits every day of the year.

He had thought about Cora's strange manner as he sat looking out of the bus window on his way to work. "Did I **rub her the wrong way** with something I said?" he asked himself. No, it couldn't be that. One thing about Cora; if she didn't like something he said, she let him know it. However, once she had done so, she **let bygones be bygones** and everything was all right again. She was always ready to **meet him halfway** when they had an argument, too—which was seldom. No, today was different. But why?

Once at the office Alex became absorbed in his work and forgot his wife's strange manner. Not until later, in Hartman's Department Store, did he think of it again. The beautiful ruby-red bowl reminded him. Suddenly he felt he had to buy this lovely piece of glassware for his wife. Surely it would help her forget whatever was bothering her. He loved Cora very much and didn't want anything in the world to make her sad. **As far as Alex was concerned,** making Cora happy was his first responsibility.

He could hardly wait to get home and sat holding the gift-wrapped bowl carefully on his knees. Why did the bus move so slowly? He was sorry he hadn't had enough money to buy the little bowls that accompanied the big one. He would have had, if he hadn't invited one of his friends to lunch that noon. Usually they **went Dutch,** but today, for some unknown reason, he had insisted on paying the restaurant check. Oh, well, he would get Cora the other dishes later. Besides, the one dish made such a big package that the man sitting next to Alex had to move over and **make room for him.**

Alex smiled to himself as he pictured Cora's face. She would tell him he was being too extravagant, especially when it wasn't even Christmas or her birthday.

When he got off the bus, Alex hurried to the house, practically running all the way. A few minutes later, Cora, opening the front door, almost fainted when Alex immediately handed her the package. "You're all **dressed up!**" Alex exclaimed. "You look beautiful!"

Cora tried to speak, but the words wouldn't come out. When at last they did, she whispered, "Oh Alex! I was sure you'd forgotten!"

"Forgotten?"

"I should have known better. You're always so thoughtful. Still, this morning when you left without saying one word about what day this is, I couldn't help feeling a little unhappy. Now I realize you acted that way **on purpose,** just to confuse me. Well, you certainly succeeded because I really **got mixed up.** I wasn't sure what day it was myself."

She began to open the package, and Alex tried to remember what day it was.

"Oh! It's beautiful! The most beautiful bowl I've ever seen!" she said. "No wife ever had a more wonderful surprise on her wedding anniversary!"

"I tried to choose something **in keeping with** the occasion," Alex replied weakly as she kissed him.

So that was it! Of course! This was their fifth wedding

anniversary. He'd **lost track of** the date. **Little did he think** he'd ever forget such an important day, but he did. Maybe, some day, he would tell Cora the truth. Right now it didn't seem a very kind thing to do. In the future he might not be so lucky as this time. Well, he would just have to **turn over a new leaf. From now on** he'd have to **pay more attention** to the calendar. He'd **keep his fingers crossed** with hope that he'd never forget their anniversary again!

## QUESTIONS ABOUT THE READING

1. Why did Alex leave work at five o'clock? Did he usually leave at that hour?
2. Why did he go to the glassware department?
3. Did he buy the little dishes to go with the big bowl? Why or why not?
4. Why did Alex and Cora like the place where they lived?
5. Had they been married very long? How long?
6. What was Cora's attitude on the morning of the story?
7. Did Alex worry about his wife all day? Why or why not?
8. Why did he buy the red bowl?
9. Did Alex tell Cora the truth?
10. Have you ever had an experience like Alex Jackson's? Tell about it.

# UNIT V

## DRILL 21

### DIALOGUE

A: Can you **give me a hand** with this desk? I want to move it.

B: Sure. Where are you going to put it?

A: On the other side of the room. I'd **made up my mind** this was the best place. But **as luck would have it,** the light is bad here. I'll have more light by the window.

B: That **makes sense.** You'll also have a good view of the city.

A: I should have put it there in the first place.

B: Well, **take hold of** the other end. It won't be hard to move.

A: I won't move it again, you can be sure of that. I'll leave it by the window **for good.**

### DEFINITIONS

**give someone a hand**   help someone
*I'll **give you a hand** when you move to your new apartment.*

**make up one's mind**   decide
> *When did you **make up your mind** to get a new car?*

**as luck would have it**   the way things happened
> *I made good notes for my speech, but **as luck would have it**, I forgot to take them with me.*

**make sense**   seem reasonable
> *I think I'll vote for Wheeler. What he says in his interviews **makes sense**.*

**take hold of something**   take in one's hands
> *I burned my hand when I **took hold of** that hot frying pan.*

**for good**   forever; permanently
> *Peter told me he's left Springfield **for good**; he'll never go back there to live again.*


## SUBSTITUTION DRILL

*Repeat the following sentences, using the substitutions listed.*

1.   Can you give me a hand with this desk?
> this table?
> the dishes?
> the children?
> these chairs?
> my homework?
> the sofa?

2.   I'd made up my mind this was the best place.
> this was the right time.
> to go to Europe for my vacation.
> to buy a new hat.
> not to buy another coat.
> not to tell them what happened.
> to sell my automobile.

3.     As luck would have it, the light was bad there.

                            his car refused to start.

                            my brother phoned that he couldn't come.

                            we were completely out of bread.

                            there wasn't time to get another.

                            she had forgotten her car keys.

                            I'd lost your address.

4.     Your idea makes sense.

    What you say

    That news article

    Frank's plan

    Professor Brown's explanation

    The politician's speech

    What Jim told us

5.     Take hold of the other end of this table.

                            the steering wheel.

                            my hand.

                            that rope.

                            Jim's arm.

                            the handle.

                            the oar.

6.     I'm going to leave the table there for good.

    He's going back to Kansas

    She's stopped eating fried foods

    Jane's given up candy

    They've gone to Alaska

    George has stopped smoking

    They're returning to Hawaii

## HOMEWORK EXERCISE

*Fill the blanks with the appropriate idioms.*

1. The governor made an excellent speech; it _____.
2. Jim isn't going to return to Washington; he's gone back to Los Angeles _____.
3. When you drive your car, you should _____ the steering wheel with both hands.
4. I have to move the sofa, but it's too big for me to move alone. Will you _____, please?
5. Alice is a person who can't make decisions; she can't _____ about anything.
6. I was very fortunate yesterday. I'd forgotten my wallet at home and didn't have any money. But, _____, I was able to borrow some from Jim.

# DRILL 22

## DIALOGUE

A: Would you like a ticket to the football game? I bought it **on the spur of the moment.** I forgot I wouldn't be in town this weekend.

B: Thanks. I'd like to go. I haven't been to any games this year.

A: You haven't missed anything. The good games have been **few and far between.** Our team hasn't played very well.

B: But they haven't done too badly. Remember, they won the last two games. I'm confident of one thing. They **have it in them** to play good football.

A: Yes, that's true. I have to admit it. At the moment they seem to be **on their toes.**

B: I'm sure that they're **bent on** winning Saturday's game.

A: Maybe **in the long run,** they'll do all right. I hope so.

# DEFINITIONS

**on the spur of the moment**  at that moment; without previous thought or plan

*I planned to study yesterday afternoon, but **on the spur of the moment** I changed my mind and went to the movies.*

**few and far between**  scarce; infrequent; rare

*Yes, I do hear from Roger, but his letters are **few and far between.***

**have it in one**  have the capacity, ability, to do something

*I think Marie **has it in her** to be a great concert pianist.*

**on one's toes**  alert

*I think Bert will get the job. He was really **on his toes** and made a good impression during the interview.*

**be bent on something**  have a strong desire to do something

*I told Harry not to drive his car in such bad weather, but **he was bent on** leaving right away.*

**in the long run**  looking ahead to the distant future, not just the near future

*You may get tired studying English every day, but **in the long run** you'll be glad that you did.*


# SUBSTITUTION DRILL

*Repeat the following sentences, using the substitutions listed.*

1.  I bought the ticket on the spur of the moment.
    Jim said yes
    Harry told us
    Alice left for Chicago

90

Jack sold his car
Tom decided to leave
John asked Mary to go with him

2. The good games have been few and far between.
His payments on the car
The worthwhile movies
His words of wisdom
Our nice summer days
Their trips to New York
Phillip's letters

3. They have it in them to play good football.
be good students.
become good singers.
earn lots of money.
win every game.
be leaders.

4. Jim's doing much better. He's really on his toes now.
Jack's
Bill's
Dick's
Frank's
Bob's

5. They seem bent on winning every game.
spending all their money.
finding hidden treasure.
telling everybody about it.
giving us their dog.
asking everyone to the party.
buying a new house.

6. In the long run they'll do all right.
we'll earn a lot of money.
she'll be glad she went.
he'll wish he'd studied.
I'll learn the truth.

they'll be sorry they did it.
she'll regret her decision.

## HOMEWORK EXERCISE

*Write a short dialogue using at least three of the idioms in this lesson. Be prepared to recite it in class with the help of one of the other students.*

# DRILL 23

## DIALOGUE

A:  I've just heard a speech by the governor. He's an excellent speaker.

B:  Yes, he's a good man. I like him. Although I don't always **see eye to eye** with him.

A:  There's one good thing about him: he isn't **behind the times.** He knows this is the twentieth century.

B:  I like the way he **got right down to** business. He's a man of action. Right from the start.

A:  That's true. He **made a point of** going to work immediately.

B:  He's very independent. He doesn't rely on others. He finds out everything **firsthand.** Then he **takes steps** to improve the situation.

A:  He's the right man for the job.

## DEFINITIONS

**see eye to eye**   to agree
*I agree with the president on domestic matters, but I don't **see eye to eye** with him on foreign policy.*

**be behind the times**   not be up-to-date, modern in one's thinking

> *He's not a good teacher. He's **behind the times** in his methods.*

**get right down to something**   begin working without hesitation

> *After the chairman opened the meeting, the committee **got right down to business.***

**make a point of something**   do or say something with a definite intention

> *When Professor Gray greeted me, he **made a point of** asking how my parents were.*

**firsthand**   without assistance from an intermediary; direct

> *What I'm telling you is **firsthand** information; I didn't hear it from someone else.*

**take steps**   prepare for something and put it into action

> *The crime in that city became a serious problem. The police had to **take steps** to correct it.*


## SUBSTITUTION DRILL

*Repeat the following sentences, using the substitutions listed.*

1.   I don't always see eye to eye with the governor.
                        the president.
                        the mayor.
                        that newspaper.
                        the teacher.
                        your brother.
                        my wife.

2. The governor isn't behind the times.
    Jack
    George
    Bill
    Frank
    Mary
    The president

3. I like the way he got right down to business.
    the mayor
    the committee
    the United Nations
    the board of directors
    Congress
    the teacher

4. He made a point of going right to work.
    learning everybody's name.
    remembering to call me.
    signing all the letters.
    telling us to come.
    looking at it himself.
    sending his car for us.

5. He learns everything he can firsthand.
    He gets all his information
    He found out all about it
    They learned how to do it
    She studied the details
    I always try to learn things
    We do best when we study things

6. The mayor took steps to do better.
    improve his methods.
    learn the truth.
    get the real facts.
    investigate the situation.

modernize the city.

form a good government.

*Write substitution drills for three idioms in this lesson. Make four substitutions for each idiom.*

# DRILL 24

## DIALOGUE

A: I'd hate to **be in Jack's shoes.** He lost his job.

B: What happened?

A: As you know, Jack's an accountant. Last month he made an error in his books. The company lost a lot of money.

B: That's a shame. Well, I'm sure of one thing: he wasn't trying to **get away with anything.**

A: Of course not. Jack's very honest. He **bent over backwards** to correct his mistake. But it was too late. To make things worse, his wife **came down with** the flu.

B: Poor Jack! How's he going to **make ends meet?**

A: I don't know. If you hear of a job, let him know. He's ready to **try his hand** at anything.

## DEFINITIONS

**be in someone's shoes**    be in another person's position
*I wish I were **in John's shoes**. He just won a free trip to Europe.*

95

**get away with something**   do something one shouldn't and not be caught at it

>   *Dave may have been successful in fooling the boss this time, but he can't **get away with it** every time.*

**bend over backwards**   try very hard; make a real effort

>   *I **bent over backwards** to help Bertha find a job, but she didn't appreciate it.*

**come down with**   become ill with

>   *I don't feel very well; I think I'm **coming down with** the flu.*

**make ends meet**   be able to live with the money one has

>   *The Smiths have seven children, and although Joe doesn't have a big salary, they seem to **make ends meet**.*

**try one's hand at something**   see if one is able to do something that requires some skill, ability

>   *I've never driven a tractor before, but I'm willing to **try my hand at it**.*


## SUBSTITUTION DRILL

*Repeat the following sentences, using the substitutions listed.*

1.   I'd hate to be in Jack's shoes.

>   Mary's
>   Mr. Black's
>   Frank's
>   Jane's
>   Pat's
>   Bob's

2.   He wasn't trying to get away with anything.
>   They weren't trying

I don't believe they wanted
No one thinks they expected
We doubt they tried
I can't imagine she would try
He never once tried

3. Jack's wife came down with the flu.
   - a bad cold.
   - malaria.
   - a sore throat.
   - bronchitis.
   - pneumonia.
   - hepatitis.

4. He bent over backwards to correct his mistake.
   - teach us English.
   - find us a better copy.
   - send his child to school.
   - do the best job he could.
   - arrive at seven o'clock.
   - get to class on time.

5. How's he going to make ends meet?
   How are they
   How are you
   How is Mary
   How is Jim
   How are the Whites
   How is Alex

6. He's ready to try his hand at anything.
   - teaching English.
   - waiting tables.
   - bookkeeping.
   - selling door-to-door.
   - writing advertising.
   - picking fruit.

## HOMEWORK EXERCISE

*Answer the following questions:*

1. Did you ever bend over backwards to do something?
2. Have you ever had trouble making ends meet?
3. When was the last time you came down with something?
4. Tell about one time when you tried your hand at something new.
5. Did you ever try to get away with something? Were you successful?

# DRILL 25

## DIALOGUE

A: Fred is remarkable! There isn't much he doesn't know.

B: I think it's his natural curiosity. He wants to know everything. He doesn't just **scratch the surface,** either. He really **gets to the bottom of** things.

A: Do you know what he explained to me today? **The ins and outs** of the stock market. He knows all about Wall Street.

B: I have to confess something. I didn't think much of Fred **at first.**

A: I understand. He's very quiet. He doesn't make a good first impression. But he **grows on you** after a while.

B: He's **a far cry from** his brother. Pete talks all the time and doesn't say anything, either.

A: There are too many Petes in the world.

B: And not enough Freds.

# DEFINITIONS

**scratch the surface**   study something superficially
> *I don't know much about international politics; I've only scratched the surface.*

**get to the bottom of something**   learn all the facts about something
> *I've made a mistake in my calculations, but I can't find it. Perhaps if I begin again and study each detail carefully, I'll get to the bottom of it.*

**the ins and outs**   all the facts about something
> *In order to learn the ins and outs of the family business, Bill took a job as messenger boy in one of the offices.*

**(not) think much of something, someone**   (used in the negative) have a good opinion of (affirmative: think a lot of)
> *I liked the book very much, although I didn't think much of the ending.*

**a far cry from something**   very different; almost the opposite
> *The movie was good, but it was a far cry from the book it was based on.*

**grow on someone**   increase in favor with someone gradually
> *I hated Kansas City at first, but I have to admit it's grown on me.*

## SUBSTITUTION DRILL

*Repeat the following sentences, using the substitutions listed.*

1.   Fred learns all the facts; he doesn't just scratch the surface.
     Bob gets all the facts;

John examines everything closely;
Paul studies everything carefully;
Robert investigates all the details;
Alex finds out all he can about something;
George looks into everything minutely;

2.  He really gets to the bottom of things.
                                   problems.
                                   difficulties.
                                   what is causing an ill-
                                     ness.
                                   why a child can't learn to
                                     read.
                                   how a machine functions.
                                   where his students have
                                     trouble learning.

3.  He explained the ins and outs of the stock market to me.
                                   the United Nations
                                   U.S. foreign policy
                                   the missile program
                                   atomic energy
                                   international relations
                                   his business

4.  I didn't think much of Fred at first.
                                   when I met him.
                                   when he told Mary to be
                                     quiet.
                                   when he acted so childish.
                                   when he became angry yes-
                                     terday.
                                   when he refused to let Jim
                                     drive his car.
                                   when he answered Martha
                                     so discourteously.

5. He's a far cry from his brother.

> what he should be.
>
> a good student.
>
> the right man for the job.
>
> my idea of a president.
>
> his father.
>
> what he promised to be.

6. Fred grew on me as I got to know him better.

Bill

Richard

Professor Allen

Dr. Burns

Chester

Paul

## HOMEWORK EXERCISE

*Fill in the blanks.*

1. I didn't like the movie. It was a _____ from the book.

2. When Mary came to work in our office, we didn't like her, but now we do; she's _____ us.

3. Alice knows _____ of the entire organization, so we asked her to explain it to us.

4. I'm having trouble with this chapter in my economics book. I've read it three times but I still don't understand it. I can't _____ .

5. Jim is always saying unkind things about Frank; he doesn't _____ him.

6. Will you read this article for me, please, and write a report? Read it carefully; don't just _____ .

# READING V

## WHAT HAPPENED IN GRIMSBY

The little town of Grimsby had a problem and no one knew what to do about it. Bert Carston was leaving.

It isn't easy to explain Bert's position in the town. Not even the citizens themselves really knew, but now that he planned to go away, they realized there was going to be a vacancy impossible to fill.

Bert was capable of doing a wide variety of tasks; he knew **the ins and outs** of thousands of different jobs. Actually, Bert had a small shop on Main Street. It was called "The Fixit Shop" and Bert was known as "Mr. Fixit." There was nothing he could not repair; his service was excellent and his prices were low.

But Bert Carston was much more than a repairman. More important than his excellent service was Bert himself. He was a friendly fellow who listened patiently while his customers told him their troubles; he often "fixed" their problems, too.

Bert was always ready to **give someone a hand;** he helped one man with a big family get a better job, because the man couldn't **make ends meet** with the one he had; if someone had no money, he would lend some; he found a quick way to relieve Main Street's congestion the day a big windstorm blew many trees down and they fell in the way of automobiles. He soon had everyone along the street organized and **taking hold of** the branches and pulling them out of the street.

The subjects that Bert was unable to discuss were **few and far between.** He was always able to reply correctly to questions about science, philosophy, or literature, and **on the spur of the moment,** too, without turning to a reference book.

In politics he could argue equally well with a liberal or a conservative and cause either to **see eye to eye** with him. He had a remarkable memory and could quote pages from Shakespeare perfectly. The reason was that Bert didn't just **scratch the surface** of a subject; he **got to the bottom** of things and he got his information **firsthand.**

One winter Bert **came down with** influenza and was sick in bed for a week. This caused problems for all those people of Grimsby who needed work done by Bert. Also, the engineer at the electrical plant had gone out of town unexpectedly, and Bert was the only one who knew what to do in case of an emergency. Of course, that was the time something went wrong. Bert should not have left the house, but he got out of bed and went to the electrical plant, repaired what was wrong, and returned home. This was very typical of Bert Carston.

Because the townspeople loved and respected Bert so much, they had one great concern for him: they felt this bachelor should be married. "A man your age shouldn't be living all alone in that little house," one of his neighbors said. "Your life is **a far cry** from what it could be with the right woman at your side."

Bert agreed but there wasn't much he could do about it. He was fifty years old and there were no eligible women his age in Grimsby. One afternoon when a little old lady known to everyone as "Grandma" Tompkins came into his shop, she **made a point of** saying, "Bert Carston, are you going to be like your father? He didn't marry until late in life."

Bert smiled. "I know, Grandma, but there's no one here in Grimsby I can marry."

"Then go to another town to find a wife. You've got an automobile, haven't you? Use it."

Why not? What Grandma said **made sense.** He should have thought of it himself.

Bert began visiting nearby towns on weekends to see if he could meet some nice woman who would like to be his wife. It took a long time and visits to many towns, but at last he found just the person he wanted. She was a widow, just a year younger than Bert. Her name was Ida Clark and she lived in Easton, only thirty-five miles from Grimsby.

Bert's friends and customers were delighted when they learned the news of his forthcoming marriage. They agreed that Ida was just the wife for Bert. It was true that she didn't make a strong first impression but, as someone said, "She **grows on** you."

Their delight ended very quickly, however. Bert announced one day that he'd **made up his mind** to move to Easton after the wedding. The people of Grimsby were shocked. "You can't do this to us!" they insisted. They became quite angry. Suddenly Bert felt that everyone in town **had it in for him.** They made him feel guilty, as though he'd tried to **get away with something.**

When asked why Ida didn't move to Grimsby instead of his going to Easton, Bert replied, "There are several reasons. First, she has a beautiful big home there, and I have a very small house here. Second, the man who has the repair shop in Easton is retiring; there will be an excellent place for me."

"But we need you here, Bert!" his friends cried.

"Young Willie Adams has been helping me here in the shop, and he's very good," Bert replied.

The people didn't **think much of** Bert's excuse. "It isn't the same. Willie may be good at repairing our radios and lamps, but he can't do the many other things you do for us."

The more the people of Grimsby thought about it, the more disturbed they became. They remembered all that Bert had done for them through the years. They had not realized until now just how important he was to the town. No one could take his place.

The day of the wedding drew near. The people still refused to believe that Bert intended to leave them. "I'll only be thirty-five miles away," he reminded them. "And I'll come back to Grimsby often. It isn't as though I was going away **for good.**"

"It isn't the same," the people insisted.

**As luck would have it,** Grandma Tompkins was away visiting her daughter in St. Louis, Missouri. She did not know any of the news about Bert and Ida. When she returned home to Grimsby, she found the entire town in a very depressed state. Grandma was the type always to **get right down to business.** "Tell me what's wrong," she demanded. The towns-people quickly explained.

"We've **bent over backwards** to persuade Bert he should stay," they said.

The old lady sat thinking quietly for a long time before she spoke. Finally she said, "Grimsby's real problem is that it isn't **on its toes.** It's quite **behind the times.** Bert's right to leave. If I were **in his shoes,** I'd leave too."

They looked at Grandma as though they had not heard correctly.

"For many years," she went on, "we have been a quiet little village and have done very well without need of a municipal government. Now we're no longer a village.

Grimsby is growing larger every year. We need a mayor. We should **take steps** to get one."

"A mayor for Grimsby?"

"Certainly. And can you think of a better man for the job than Bert Carston?"

"But Bert is leaving!"

Grandma had a look of disgust on her face. "Do you think he'd move away if he were elected mayor of Grimsby?"

Smiles returned to the faces of the citizens as they realized what she was suggesting. "Of course! Bert can't move away if he's our mayor. Let's have an election right away!"

The problem was solved. The townspeople held a public meeting. Bert Carston was unanimously elected the first mayor of Grimsby. There was nothing he could do but agree to stay. Ida sold her house and moved to Grimsby. "You can't leave Grimsby now," she told Bert. "You have to stay. Besides, I like the idea of being a mayor's wife."

Bert smiled. "It might be fun to **try my hand** at being a mayor."

Grandma Tompkins smiled, too. "If there isn't one way to solve a problem," she told the people of Grimsby, "there's always another; if you're really **bent on** finding a solution, that is. You just have to be patient and continue trying. **In the long run** you'll find a way."

## QUESTIONS ABOUT THE READING

1. Why was Bert Carston called "Mr. Fixit"?
2. What did the people of Grimsby keep telling Bert he should do?
3. Why did Bert know so many details about things?
4. Who was Grandma Tompkins? What did she tell Bert he should do?

5. Who was Ida Clark? Where did she live?
6. What did Bert tell his friends that shocked them?
7. Where was Grandma Tompkins when Bert decided to marry Ida?
8. What was Grandma's solution to Grimsby's problem?
9. Did Grandma's idea work? How?
10. Do you agree with Grandma that there's always a solution to every problem?

# UNIT VI

## DRILL 26

### DIALOGUE

A: I always **bite off more than I can chew**. I agreed to speak at the club next Monday. Now I won't be able to do it.

B: Why not? What happened?

A: I'm going to Denver that day. I forgot all about it. I don't **have the heart** to tell the club now. It's the second time I've done this. How can I **save face**?

B: Don't worry about it. They'd have to search **high and low** to find a better speaker. And they know it.

A: Thank you. But I doubt that. I'm sure they'd prefer someone who **keeps his word**.

B: Forget it. They know you're not **leading them on**. They'll ask you again, I'm sure.

### DEFINITIONS

**bite off more than one can chew**   try to do more than one is able to; accept more responsibility than one can take care of
  *When Jim accepted the presidency of the club, he **bit off more than he could chew**.*

108

**(not) have the heart** (usually used in the negative)   have the courage to do something that will cause others unhappiness or disappointment

> *Alfred failed his exam, but his teacher **doesn't have the heart** to tell him.*

**save face**   maintain one's pride and honor; not be disgraced

> *Donald completely forgot Irene's party and tried to **save face** by sending her flowers the next morning.*

**high and low**   everywhere; in every conceivable place

> *I've lost my passport. I've looked **high and low** for it, but I can't find it.*

**keep one's word**   be responsible and do what one says one will do

> *If Paul said he'd get that book for you, he'll do it; he always **keeps his word**.*

**lead someone on**   make someone believe something that isn't true

> *Alec gave me a long story about what a good student he was in college. Later I discovered none of it was true; he was just **leading me on**.*


## SUBSTITUTION DRILL

*Repeat the following sentences, using the substitutions listed.*

1.   I always bite off more than I can chew.
        often
        frequently
        usually
        sometimes
        never
        seldom

2.  I don't have the heart to tell the members I won't be there.

> my wife
> Helen
> my boss
> them
> Ida
> Richard

3.  They'd have to search high and low to find a better speaker.

> anyone bet-
> ter prepared.
> a finer
>   pianist.
> brighter stu-
> dents
> harder
>   workers.
> nicer
>   weather.
> a prettier
>   garden.

4.  We want someone who keeps his word.

> need
> prefer
> respect
> insist on
> demand
> would like

5.  How can I save face?

> he
> she
> they
> we

110

Mary
George

6. They know you aren't leading them on.
     understand
     realize
     are grateful
     are confident
     feel sure
     are certain

## HOMEWORK EXERCISE

*Tell the class an expression in your language, translated into English literally, which conveys the same idea, or a similar idea, as the following idioms:*

bite off more than one can chew _____

keep one's word _____

have the heart _____

save face _____

high and low _____

lead someone on _____

# DRILL 27

## DIALOGUE

A: What's wrong with Jerry? I was with him in the coffee shop this noon. He was in good spirits. We were talking and laughing. Then Barbara came in. Suddenly Jerry was **ill at ease.**

B: Didn't you know? They had a quarrel yesterday. Jerry **made fun of** Barbara's hat.

A: Is that all? She doesn't **hold that against him,** does she?

B: No, I don't think so. But you know Barbara. She's quite particular about her appearance. Well, she **lost her temper.** Now she won't speak to Jerry.

A: I'd better have a talk with Barbara. She's being childish. That's nothing to **get on her high horse** about.

B: I'll bet Jerry could **eat his words** now. He'll be careful what he says about ladies' hats!


## DEFINITIONS

**ill at ease**   not comfortable psychologically
*David speaks easily in front of a small group but he seems **ill at ease** before a large audience.*

**make fun of something, someone**   ridicule, laugh at
*I've decided that the reason Jim always **makes fun of** others is that he's so insecure himself.*

**hold something against someone**   blame someone for something for a period of time
*I was responsible for Fred's being late to class this morning, but he doesn't **hold it against me**.*

**lose one's temper**   become angry
*When Sam's wife told him she'd had an accident with the car, he **lost his temper**.*

**get on one's high horse**   become angry and superior in attitude toward someone else
*Vernon is a Republican, and he **gets on his high horse** every time someone criticizes his party*

**eat one's words**   admit one is wrong in something one has said
*Richard insisted the United States was larger than Bra-*

*zil, but he had to **eat his words** when Elizabeth showed him the map.*

## SUBSTITUTION DRILL

*Repeat the following sentences, using the substitutions listed.*

1. Jerry seemed ill at ease when Barbara came in.

   Alice
   his boss
   his mother-in-law
   Pauline
   Frieda
   the girls

2. He made fun of Barbara's hat.

   Henry's coat.
   the teacher's accent.
   Mae's dress.
   Paul's handwriting.
   Marian's voice.
   the governor's speech.

3. Does Barbara hold Jerry's tardiness against him?

   sense of humor
   way of speaking
   manner of dressing
   actions last night
   bad behavior
   overeating

4. She lost her temper. Now she won't speak to Jerry.

   Now she won't go with us.
   Now she won't do that typing.
   Now she won't take the medicine.
   Now she won't write my letter.
   Now she won't tell us what happened.

5. It's ridiculous for Barbara to get on her high horse about
   that.
   Jerry's driving.
   Bill's politics.
   your clothes.
   Frank's decision.
   what you said.
   Harry's joke.

6. I'll bet Jerry could eat his words now.
   I imagine
   I don't doubt
   I'm sure
   I feel certain
   I have a feeling
   I've no doubt that

## HOMEWORK EXERCISE

*Tell about a time when you*

1. lost your temper
2. felt ill at ease
3. had to eat your words
4. got on your high horse

# DRILL 28

## DIALOGUE

A: No one in our club works harder than Jeanne. She's always glad to **do her bit.**

B: All organizations are like that. A few members do everything. The other just want to have fun.

A: Of course, Jeanne prefers it that way. She's **in her element** when she's working hard.

B: Her sister Rita is quite different. She **comes up with** excellent ideas. But she never **carries them out.** Even when Jeanne **gets after her.**

A: There's a special meeting at the club tonight. Are you going?

B: I can't. I already have another meeting to attend. **Remember me to everyone** if you go.


## DEFINITIONS

**do one's bit**   fulfill one's responsibility to; help accomplish something
> *If everyone who offered to help would come and **do his bit,** we could finish this job in an hour.*

**in one's element**   doing something one likes and is capable of doing very well
> *Look at Norman! He's **in his element** when he's arguing politics!*

**come up with**   suggest; contribute; introduce
> *When the teacher asked what the capital of California was, only one student could **come up with** the right city.*

**get after someone**   tell someone to do something you feel he should do
> *Every time Professor Jackson goes out into the rain, his wife has to **get after him** to carry his umbrella.*

**carry something out**   fulfill; see that something is done
> *One good thing about Clarence; he not only has good ideas, but he **carries them out,** too.*

115

**remember someone to someone else**   tell someone to say hello to another person for you

   *Remember me to your brother when you see him.*


## SUBSTITUTION DRILL

*Repeat the following sentences, using the substitutions listed.*

1. Jeanne is always glad to do her bit.
   Mary's always delighted
   Phyllis is happy
   Nancy can be counted on
   Patricia never fails
   Marie has promised
   Eva says she'll try

2. She's in her element when she's working hard.
                              teaching English.
                              studying languages.
                              cleaning house.
                              baking pies.
                              cooking stew.
                              knitting a sweater.

3. Rita comes up with excellent ideas.
                       fresh ideas.
                       interesting observations.
                       intelligent comments.
                       funny remarks.
                       unusual words.
                       brilliant thoughts.

4. She never carries out her ideas.
                         her plans.
                         her promises.

our programs.

Bill's suggestions.

his orders.

my requests.

5. Jeanne gets after her to work.

study.

practice English.

exercise.

sing in the chorus.

take up painting.

6. Please remember me to everyone.

your wife.

your brother.

Alex and Anne.

the Browns.

your sister.

Professor Miller.

## HOMEWORK EXERCISE

*Fill in the blanks.*

1. Jim's parents are always _____ to do his homework.

2. When everyone does _____ , the work isn't difficult.

3. When Bill finds someone who likes golf, he's really _____ .

4. Rita _____ a brilliant idea for the club's next party.

5. Jack has good suggestions, but he never _____ .

6. Are you going to see John? Please _____ .

# DRILL 29

A:  Tell me exactly what Bob said. Don't **beat around the bush.** Give it to me **straight from the shoulder.**

B:  **Hold your horses!** I'll tell you in a minute. Let me **catch my breath.**

A:  You can do that later. Tell me. What did Bob say?

B:  Do you really want to know?

A:  Of course I do.

B:  Okay. If you really want to know. He said you always try to **pull the wool over his eyes.**

A:  What? That's not true! Perhaps I exaggerate a little. But that's all. I've never tried to deceive him.

B:  Why don't you do what I do?

A:  What's that?

B:  **Take his remark with a grain of salt.**


## DEFINITIONS

**beat around the bush**    speak indirectly, evasively
  *I wish Albert would say what he really means and not always* **beat around the bush.**

**straight from the shoulder**    frankly
  *I prefer a person who speaks* **straight from the shoulder,** *because then I know exactly what he means.*

**hold one's horses**    wait patiently instead of going forward
  *When Betty insisted that they leave immediately, Jeff told her to* **hold her horses,** *since there was plenty of time before their plane left.*

**catch one's breath**   rest for a moment
> *When Mrs. Brewster reached the top of the hill, she was so tired she had to stop for a moment and **catch her breath**.*

**pull the wool over someone's eyes**   deceive someone
> *Ethel was sure that Robert was **pulling the wool over her eyes** when he said he'd been in the library studying all evening.*

**take something with a grain of salt**   only half believe something someone has said
> *Jack is a very likable fellow, but I've learned to **take everything he says with a grain of salt**.*


SUBSTITUTION DRILL

*Repeat the following sentences, using the substitutions listed.*

1.  Tell me the truth! Don't beat around the bush.
    Come to the point!
    Be truthful now!
    Tell us what happened!
    Repeat every word!
    Answer me honestly!
    Be direct!
2.  Give it to me straight from the shoulder.
    > us
    > them
    > her
    > him
    > George
    > Eleanor

3.   Hold your horses. I'll tell you in a minute.
                    I'll explain everything.
                    I'll answer all your questions.
                    I'll find your book for you.
                    I'll get your money right now.
                    I'll sign the papers soon.
                    I'll tell them what happened.

4.   Let me catch my breath before I tell you.
                    answer.
                    go any further.
                    explain what happened.
                    run any farther.
                    try to speak.
                    reply.

5.   He said you tried to pull the wool over his eyes.
          she
          Bob
          they
          Alice
          we
          I

6.   Take it with a grain of salt. That's what Bob does.
                    That's the wise thing.
                    That's the best way.
                    That's what I do.
                    That's more sensible.
                    That's more realistic.
                    That's what I suggest.

## HOMEWORK EXERCISE

*Answer these questions.*

1.   Do you like people who speak straight from the shoulder?

120

2. How do you express the idea of "Hold your horses!" in your language?

3. Why do people often beat around the bush?

4. Did you ever try to pull the wool over someone's eyes?

5. Do you think it's a good idea to take what other people say with a grain of salt?

6. Do you have to catch your breath after you climb a hill?


# DRILL 30

## DIALOGUE

A: I'm sorry to keep you waiting. I'll **make short work of** this.

B: **Take your time.** I'm in no hurry.

A: **It's always up to me** to see that the office is closed.

B: Every night?

A: Yes, and I usually close at 5:30. **Once in a blue moon** I have to stay late. This is one of those times.

B: You really **know the ropes** around here.

A: Well, I should. I've been here ten years. You have to **take that into account.**

B: You're very modest. I'm sure your boss must be pleased with your work.


## DEFINITIONS

**make short work of something**   do something quickly
*The thief **made short work** of robbing the bank.*

**take one's time**   do something slowly; not hurry
*When you're eating, it's important to **take your time** and chew your food well.*

**something is up to someone**   it is one's responsibility to take care of something or to make a decision

> *Tom said it was **up to** Anne to choose the movie they should see that evening.*

**once in a blue moon**   very infrequently; almost never

> *I seldom see Bill. Only **once in a blue moon**.*

**know the ropes**   be very familiar with routine procedures such as those of a business, factory, or school

> *I'll enjoy my new job more as soon as **I know the ropes**.*

**take something into account**   consider something

> *In considering Andy for the job, we must **take into account** that he has very bad eyesight.*


## SUBSTITUTION DRILL

*Repeat the following sentences, using the substitutions listed.*

1.   Sorry to keep you waiting. I'll make short work of this.
     Excuse me for making you wait.
     Pardon me for taking so long.
     I'm sorry you have to wait.
     Sorry I made you wait.
     Excuse me for delaying you.
     Pardon me for making a mistake.
2.   Take your time. I'm in no hurry.
                      I'm not going anywhere.
                      I have nothing to hurry for.
                      I have nothing to do.
                      I have all day.
                      I have more time than money.
                      I don't have to go anywhere.

3.     It's up to me to close the office every night.
                                 see that the lights are out.
                                 take care of the building.
                                 get coffee for everyone.
                                 write these letters.
                                 take charge of the meeting.
                                 tell them what happened.

4.     Once in a blue moon I'm late.
                                 he's early.
                                 they're on time.
                                 she telephones me.
                                 we go out to dinner.
                                 Jim writes me a letter.
                                 I get a bad cold.

5.     You really know the ropes in this office.
                                      your department.
                                      this company.
                                    this organization.
                                    this club.
                                    that society.
                                    your factory.

6.     You must take into account that I've been here ten years.
                                           I'm older than Tom.
                                       she's his sister.
                                        they're well informed.
                                     he's from Brazil.
                                   we're students.
                                   he's only a child.


## HOMEWORK EXERCISE

*Write a paragraph using at least three of the idioms in this lesson.*

# READING VI

## THE MAN WITH THE SCAR

When Detective Paul Nichols asked the teller at the Middleton Bank to describe the robber, she replied. "He had a long, ugly scar on his right cheek. Also, he seemed quite **ill at ease,** as though he might be unsure of what he was doing. But he did it. I had the feeling, though, that he went through with it almost just to **save face.** Once he decided to rob the bank, he had to **carry out** his plan."

She explained that the man had come into the bank that morning and stood in line with the other customers, as if waiting to deposit money or cash a check. When he reached the window, however, he did not **beat around the bush;** he handed the girl a piece of paper that had written on it, "Do not say anything or do anything unusual. I have a gun and will use it if I have to. Put five thousand dollars in an envelope and hand it to me."

The girl was so shocked that she just stood looking at him for a moment. She realized he was not joking; what he ordered was **straight from the shoulder.** He said he would use his gun if he had to, and she was sure he would **keep his word** if she didn't cooperate. The teller did exactly as he told her.

**"Remember me to your mother,"** the thief said. Then he walked casually out of the bank. Not even the lady behind him in line at the window realized what had happened.

The teller sounded the alarm, and immediately the guards ran to find the thief. "You can't mistake him with that scar," the girl told them. "But be careful. He has a gun."

A thorough search was made, but no such person was found. The guards couldn't even **come up with** a piece of evidence.

"I can't understand how he could get away so rapidly," Detective Nichols told his wife Nancy that evening, as the two of them were having supper. "We questioned everyone inside and outside the bank at the time of the robbery. No one saw a man with a scar on his face.

"The guard at the door sees everyone who goes in and out, but he doesn't recall anyone with a scar. It looks as though the man appeared from nowhere and returned to nowhere. At least, for the moment it seems so."

"He came from somewhere and he went somewhere when he left the bank," Nancy replied. "The question is, where did he go?" Nancy Nichols was a very practical woman. Her husband liked to discuss his cases with her because of this trait.

Paul continued. "The girl was surprised because it all happened within a few seconds, and so smoothly. She just stood watching the man walk away. When he went out the door, her senses returned to her and she called the guard."

"What time of day was it?" Nancy asked.

"Noon. The streets were filled with people. At that hour of the day, it's always that way in front of the Middleton Bank. He could get lost in the crowd very easily. The men on the police force insist he just disappeared."

"With a scar on his face? **I take that with a grain of salt.** He didn't disappear; you can be sure of that. But what did he do?" Nancy began to have an expression of real excitement in her eyes. She was **in her element** when helping Paul solve a case. She loved to **do her bit** and resented it when Paul didn't consult with her. After ten years of being a detective's wife, she ought to **know the ropes**—and she did. This was the type of case she enjoyed most.

"That's what is so confusing. We looked **high and low** and questioned everyone in the area at the time of the robbery but no one observed anything or anyone unusual. Several people admitted they saw a man come out of the bank about that time, but he didn't have a scar on his face." Paul shook his head and sighed wearily. It had been a tiring day and a mystifying case. **Once in a blue moon** Paul had a case that seemed impossible to solve. This was one of them. And it **was up to** Paul to solve it.

"Don't worry," Nancy encouraged him. "In the end you'll find your thief."

When supper was over, the Nichols had their coffee in the living room. Paul turned on the television set and immediately became interested in a detective program. Nancy did not watch the program but sat drinking her coffee in silence. When she had finished, she went into the kitchen and began washing the dishes.

Fifteen minutes later she returned to the living room. She went directly to the television set and turned it off.

"What are you doing?" Paul objected, almost **losing his temper**. "It's a very exciting story tonight!"

"Have you **taken into account**," Nancy asked, ignoring his annoyance, "the possibility that the thief wanted the teller to see his scar, that he was just **leading her on**?"

"What? But why?" asked Paul, immediately forgetting the TV show. "Why should he want her to see it? It would be an excellent way to describe him. Just the opposite. He would want to hide the scar."

"As you say, it's an excellent way to describe him. And that's exactly what he wanted. He wanted her to describe him just as she did. That way, the police would be looking for a man with a scar on his right cheek."

Paul shook his head again. "What are you trying to say, Nancy?"

126

She did not reply. Instead she simply peeled off one of her false eyelashes.

For a moment Paul sat staring at her, more confused than ever. Nancy's false eyelashes were one of the few things the Nichols ever argued about. Paul tried to discourage her using false eyelashes by **making fun** of them. "I like your eyes the way Nature made them," he told her. He was always **getting after her** to leave her eyes alone and not try to make her lashes artificially longer. But sometimes she wore the lashes anyway. "I like them," she gave as her reason.

Now she was standing in front of him deliberately removing them. What was this all about? They were talking about the man with the scar and . . .

"Of course!" he shouted, jumping up from his chair. "Why didn't *I* think of that?"

Five minutes later he was in his car, hurrying to the police station.

**"Hold your horses!"** Chief Simpson said when Paul tried to tell him all at once what Nancy had discovered. "Now, begin again and this time **take your time.**"

Paul **caught his breath** and started again, more calmly.

The chief of police listened closely as Detective Nichols revealed his wife's discovery. When Paul had finished, the chief turned on his radio. "Calling all cars! Calling all cars!" He gave a detailed description of the man with the scar. Except that this time he did not mention a scar.

The police **made short work of** capturing him; they had their man within twenty-four hours. Shortly afterward they had his confession.

He was an actor without work, desperate for money. His parents were not wealthy, and the young man didn't **have the heart** to ask them for help. This was his first crime. As an actor, he knew how to disguise himself well. He was very clever. He had come into the bank with the other customers, gone to the washroom, and put a thin strip of transparent material on his cheek. The material gave the appearance of a real scar. It looked completely authentic. Then he had gone to the teller's window and taken the money. When he stopped to light a cigarette, he quickly peeled off the scar, just as Nancy had done with her false eyelash. The guard at the door and the people outside saw no one with a scar, because there was no such person.

The thief had walked quietly down the street in the middle of the noonday crowd, the money in his pocket, thinking he had **pulled the wool over the eyes of everyone.** But, unfortunately for him, he had **bitten off more than he could chew.** In the end he was caught.

Nancy smiled when Chief Simpson thanked her for her part in helping solve the mystery. "Maybe now," she laughed, "Paul will stop **getting on his high horse** about my false eyelashes."

The detective smiled, too. "Okay, okay. I'll **eat my words.** You can wear them all you want. I'll never again **hold that against you.**"

## QUESTIONS ABOUT THE READING

1. Describe what happened in the bank.
2. What time of day was it?
3. Did anyone see the man with the scar? Where did he go?
4. Who was Nancy? Did she like to help Paul solve crimes?
5. What was the one thing the Nichols argued about?
6. What did Nancy do to help solve the mystery of the man with the scar?
7. What did Paul do as soon as he realized what the man had done?
8. What did Chief Simpson do when Paul gave him the solution to the crime?
9. Did they catch the man with the scar?
10. What did Paul promise Nancy?

# INDEX

*The number following an idiom indicates the drill in which it may be found.*

130